Social Media Marketing

How Data Analytics helps to monetize the
User Base in Telecoms, Social Networks, Media
and Advertising in a Converged Ecosystem

By
Ajit Jaokar
Brian Jacobs
Alan Moore and
Jouko Ahvenainen

Copyright © Futuretext Ltd

Published by
Futuretext Ltd
36 St George St
Mayfair
London
W1S 2FW, UK
February 2009
e-mail: info@futuretext.com
www.futuretext.com

Contents

Acknowledgements

We would like to thank the following for their help and guidance with this book.

Graham Trickey, Dr Andrea Back, Dr Miguel Rio, MEP James Elles, Jag Minhas, Katrin Jordan, Tomi Ahonen, Janne Aukia, Hugo Gävert, Bettina von Kupsch, Harry Santamäki, Andrew Grill, Matthew Snyder, Christoffer Langenskiöld.

From Xtract: Janne Sinkkonen, Kimmo Kiviluoto, Mika Lindholm, and Arlinda Sipilä and Matt Dicks from Flirtomatic.

Foreword by Antti Öhrling

Engagement matters

My career in marketing, with over 25 years of experience, includes virtually all aspects of modern brand building. It encompasses FMCG marketing, direct marketing, retail marketing, publishing (print and television), as well as the advertising and online industries. Anyone with that amount of experience and with a successful career should surely be fully qualified in marketing, right?

Three years ago I became deeply involved in the telecommunications industry as a co-founder of Blyk — the first free mobile network funded by advertising. In one year we have succeeded in growing a member base of over 200,000 members in the UK without using traditional media. Net advocacy and brand preference among our members is higher than it is for all the other operators, who have to spend millions and millions of pounds on traditional advertising every year.

How is this possible? Blyk is a brand that belongs to its members, and co-creation and co-development are the strongest ways to engage them. We ask and listen to our members. A question is always a stronger way to communicate than an answer. Blyk members have become brand advocates and member-get-member is the strongest acquisition channel. Our marketing is driven entirely by social media. The phenomenon of Blyk defies all traditional models of marketing. It is a true representative of something completely new in marketing, it belongs to a new era of marketing that is more complex — but also more exciting — than ever before.

The concept of simple marketing – a phrase I use here to describe the classical view towards marketing taught by many scholars even today – is permanently over. Simple marketers apply a broadcasting mindset to marketing: We as the brand have something very important to sell and you as consumers are our "target audience", which we segment in various ways. We then bombard you with our messages, sliced and diced in bite-sized pieces to match your purchasing drivers. We measure your awareness and preferences, plan media spending carefully to optimise your exposure to our message (just the right dose, thank you!), take samples to understand what is moving inside your head (we call it market insight), tweak our value propositions or make cosmetic product face-lifts to fight off parity performance, determine various price points that open your wallets, select the best distribution channels to reach you as we see fit… we'll do nearly anything to get your attention and make you buy our product or service. Anything but engage you in a dialogue with us, as we would not know how to conduct millions of conversations simultaneously.

This one-way view of marketing and communication is partly a result of the limited options available in the media mix. Most of the media is in broadcast mode: "we talk, you listen." The rise of online has changed perceptions slightly, yet some expert views are still limited to statements such as: Television and online work well together, or WOM (word-of-mouth) can be successfully combined with increased POS (point-of-sale) communication. Forward-thinking media planners have for some time tried to apply a more holistic and integrated approach to media planning. But as media planning is based on numbers and analysis, lack of data has prevented a wider adoption of new media opportunities such as mobile and social media.

For a long time, the telecommunication industry has suffered from an inferiority complex compared with the online/internet industry. Although mobile phones have fundamentally changed the lives of nearly half the world's population, the web still has more clout. Even mobile media is struggling to establish itself adhering to natural behaviour in mobile communication. For instance, the mobile internet emphasises the word "internet" rather than "mobile". It is therefore refreshing to see that modern data analytics can best be applied to mobile telecommunications. By doing so, the telecommunication industry almost unwillingly becomes a laboratory for modern marketing science. An almost unlimited amount of raw data can be processed to improve our understanding of the underlying and complex relationships that form the foundation of "social media". The discoveries that have and will be made in the telecommunication industry will help brands and marketers in all industries.

In this book of Social Media Marketing, Ajit Jaokar, Brian Jacobs, Alan Moore and Jouko Ahvenainen open an exciting new chapter in marketing. This is a must-read book for anyone in marketing who wants to be on top of their game now and in the future. The book shows a glimpse of a new world in marketing intelligence, something we all knew existed, but could not quantify or measure. Although some of the writing covers marketing challenges that are perhaps familiar only to telecommunication industry professionals, it also provides excellent insight for other marketers. As the media landscape changes fast and dramatically towards social media, marketing methods will have to change as well. And that change has already started. Join in!

Introduction

Our approach

'Markets are conversations.'

When Doc Searls wrote those words 10 years ago, few truly understood the full dramatic extent of his observation. Yet in a recent 2008 report Nokia noted that 25% of all media will be created by us by 2012. And coupled with that we see the creation of data flows exploding from 161 billion gigabytes in 2006 to 988 billion gbs by 2012. YouTube uploads 7 hours of audio- visual content every 60 seconds of every day of the year. That's a lot of data.

We no longer live in a society governed by the simple rules of mass media, nor by the frameworks that apply to mass media production, dissemination and economics. We live in a networked society, where we, the people formerly known as the audience, are now the media. This has brought about tremendous pressure on the entire economics of the media, the marketing and the advertising industries.

In 2005, when Alan co-authored 'Communities Dominate Brands', he described at length the challenges brought about by digital economics. He discussed the generation dubbed as the 'Generation-C' – The Community Generation. The generation that has grown up connected and socially networked, wanting to engage, participate, create and co-create. He pointed to the role data and more importantly Social Marketing Intelligence, the Black Gold of the 21st Century would play in this wired 'We Media' world.

Three years on, 'Social Media', or 'Social Media Networking', accompanied by the 2.0 moniker have become familiar, if misunderstood terms. Inaccurately, the terms have become almost synonymous with enormous sites like 'My Space' and 'Facebook'. This is not what we mean by 'Social Media'. We mean any media form that links people and communities – including many smaller sites, mobile internet services and telephony.

The digitally networked visitor to these social media forms leaves behind footprints, shadows and trails of his or her individual and collective endeavours in the form of data; data that enables new type of marketing and communication between and within consumer communities. The challenge now is to harness these data flows and make money from them.

This book is interested in approaching marketing communication from a social media perspective, and in the data and analytics (from online and from mobile telecommunications sources) that allow us the opportunity to improve that process. But unlike other books, this book, is a work in progress. Thus the copy you're holding has no pretentions of being the definitive article or the one true answer to all questions on social media marketing. It provides 'AN' approach not 'THE' approach and we certainly don't claim to have all the answers.

Rather, we would like you to see this as the start of what we hope will be an engaging conversation. As a good friend once said, people will talk about you whether you like it or not, so you might as well join in the conversation.

At the end of 2008 we had sent a strictly limited edition of this book to thought leaders throughout relevant industries. We invited comments and suggestions on our website – www.social-media-marketing-community.com – some of these comments have been incorporated in this edition. In fact, some of the issues we addressed in the earlier 'BETA' edition are only now being discussed; for instance, the privacy conditions on the usage of aggregated data (as opposed to individualised data).

We will be bringing out a further edition in April or May 2009; so we encourage you to send us your comments for possible inclusion.

Our aim in writing this book has been to outline key areas that need to be highlighted and discussed as we edge towards a better understanding of social media marketing. We explore how social data flows can play a key role in all aspects of marketing, and its implications on media planning, buying and selling.

We believe that to study social media marketing, we first have to understand social media itself. Social media is an odd discipline and from the earliest times has attracted a cross-section of experts. Social media draws on Social Scientists like Manuel Castells[1] and Jan van Dijk[2] and Mathematicians like Stanley Milgram[3] and Laszlo Barabasi[4] to create a fascinating discipline which still is at an early stage in its evolution.

Taking a cue from this, we too have adopted an interdisciplinary approach, with authors from a background in research, advertising, media and data analysis. In addition, the book is based on the PhD research conducted by Ajit Jaokar. Due to the ever-evolving nature of

---

1   http://en.wikipedia.org/wiki/Manuel_Castells
2   http://en.wikipedia.org/wiki/Jan_van_Dijk
3   http://en.wikipedia.org/wiki/Stanley_Milgram
4   http://en.wikipedia.org/wiki/Albert-L%C3%A1szl%C3%B3_Barab%C3%A1si

this field, many of the ideas we have used are based on research papers. Please contact Ajit Jaokar (ajit.jaokar@futuretext.com) for a copy of his research, funded by Xtract Corporation

In this book, we introduce a set of social media metrics along with some implementation details. However, we primarily focus on the concepts and the method (algorithms) underlying social media metrics.

Our approach is data driven. It is also based on convergence (Web/ Mobile/Telecoms and Media). In this sense, it differs from other complimentary approaches due to its emphasis on data. Many of the social relationships / behavioural analysis stated here can be inferred from the underlying data. In fact, it is more insightful to derive relationships from the underlying data rather than from explicitly stated relationships.

For instance, when members register for a social network, they enter profile details. However, most check the minimum set of boxes needed to sign up. Hence, the profile information can be limited. We introduce the concept of activity driven profiles or 3D profiles which may be enriched based on user activity in the social network. This is a powerful concept and useful to both the users and advertisers. However, to implement this concept requires an understanding of the underlying data.

We approach social media marketing from three distinct but interrelated perspectives, the Web (including social media), Telecoms (including mobile) and Media. These perspectives are interconnected and based on data and conversations.

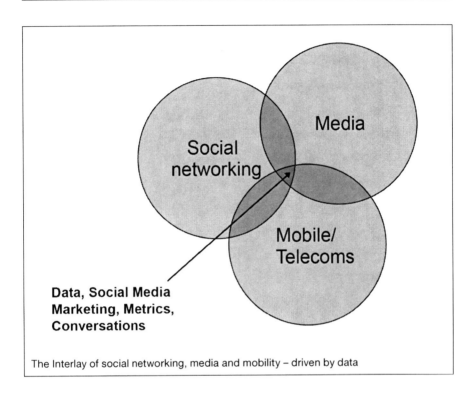

The Interlay of social networking, media and mobility – driven by data

We also describe social networking concepts without explaining the theory in great detail. We include the concept of 'The Graph Theory' in the Appendix.

Social media analytics: not data warehousing 2.0

Social media analytics is not the same as data warehousing. Two of the authors (Ajit and Jouko) come from a data warehousing/ data mining background – but social media analytics differs from traditional data warehousing in that it is oriented towards a specific function (customer conversations) and leads to social media campaigns which are iterative in nature.

Where it all began: The quest for self identity or why do we feel the need to belong to communities?

Community precedes technology – it is in fact the start of a civilisation. We have always felt the need to belong to a community. Pre-industrialisation, we were tied to our communities by geography and external forces shaped our identity. For example, if you lived in a village you would have grown, married, conducted business and died within that village. Your identity would have been completely shaped by the external forces around you and those forces would have meant that you evolved within a community defined by physical boundaries (such as a village community). The village created a community where participation was high and the skills required to participate were low.

But as industrialisation progressed, we became more mobile and urbanised and started to decouple from external forces that had shaped our identities for the millennia. Thus, our sense of identity and attachment to tight communities also changed. This happened more in western cultures (followed by other cultures in local variations). For example, from the late 1950s we witnessed a cultural revolution: Rock'n'Roll, experimentation with alternative religions, drugs, the rise of the civil rights movement, the Paris riots of 1968 etc.

Today, our identities are not constructed and defined by tradition, geography and economics and consequently we can have many selves, as we undertake a quest for **self-identity**. This is described as Psychological Self-Determination: the ability to exert control over the most important aspects of one's life, especially personal identity, which has become the source of meaning and purpose in a life no longer dictated by geography or tradition. So we are shunning traditional organisations in favour of unmediated relationships for things we care about. And we are now demanding a high quality of direct participation and influence. We have developed skills to lead, confer and discuss, and we are not content being just good foot soldiers.

Human beings are a **WE SPECIES** with an innate need to connect and communicate. And that is why social networking in all its forms is thriving. It might be worth pointing out here that new technologies do not come out of nowhere. As both William Powers, and Carlota Perez argue, new technologies are they are indeed human creations and in the first place and whether they succeed, or not, depends on to the extent to which that they meet human needs. Let's face it, if Gutenberg's printing press was deemed of no real use to society, we would not have adopted it, and we can include the inventions of Marconi, Edison, Alexander Graham Bell, and Tim Berners Lee in this. Gentlemen take a bow!

In other words, people have tremendous influence over how technologies evolve. Perez points out that at a certain point in a technology's life cycle, we the people take that technology and direct it towards very specific goals and purposes, like the tools of web 2.0 and its moniker the social media. Marshall McLuhan argues in 'The Gutenberg Galaxy' that technologies are not simply inventions which people employ but are in fact the means by which people are re-invented. Howard Rheingold, describes the technologies that we are currently creating, deploying and directing towards a common goal as 'technologies of cooperation'.

This is reflected in business, in education and in the sciences: people working together and collaborating together to achieve specific goals and tasks. So whilst the technology is new and exciting – certainly for those who value the monetising bit – it really shows an underlying truth about who we are. Even the term 'user-generated content' is a remnant of the old world as it treats participants of social networks as 'users'. A much better term is 'co-created content' or 'social content'. However 'co-creation' goes way beyond this simplistic view of something far more powerful and complex. People embrace what they create. What does this mean for brands and business? It means that, by engaging your customers in your business, more relevant solutions can be created that your most passionate customers can believe in and advocate.

> People embrace what they create. Hence, the more engaged the community is in co-creating a product or a service, the more likely it is that the final product will be accepted. This idea creates the intellectual foundation behind the notion of Engagement Marketing.

The web – an overview

The Web is organised around content. Most people start with the 'Search' option when they start using the Web. With the rise of Facebook, MySpace and other sites, online social networks have become popular and have led to the creation of what we might term as 'The Social Web'. The Social Web is organised around people (participants in a social network), as opposed to content; and we typically start our interaction with it by searching for specific people.

The content created by the participants in the Social Web has given rise to a term called as the Social Media – which is generally used to denote User Generated Content, or content created as a result of social communications. Social media might include text, video, audio and pictures.

In this book, we take a converged approach to social media spanning the Web (social networks), Media and Telecoms. When viewed in a converged and holistic manner, the two common elements which underpin social networks are:

a) The conversation between the participants in the social network

b) The data that results from the conversation.

Any body of transactional data derived from participants in an electronic conversation can be viewed as a social network (such as email data, telecoms call records, instant messaging data, forum posts etc)

This idea forms a key principle in our research for this book.

In fact, a social network can be viewed as an 'umbrella' on top of any conversational data. This approach is not new and is similar to the notion of overlay networks[5]. An overlay network is a network built on top of another network. Nodes in an overlay network can be seen to have a set of logical (virtual) links between the nodes of the base network. For instance, a Peer to Peer network[6] can be seen as an overlay network created on top of the Internet.

Overlay networks reveal new pathways and relationships between the nodes of the base network and are a reflection of the usage of the nodes. Thus, depending on function, multiple overlay networks can be built on top of the base networks – a social network for business, a social network for dating etc.

---

5   http://en.wikipedia.org/wiki/Overlay_network

6   http://en.wikipedia.org/wiki/Peer-to-peer

Whichever way we look at communication networks, one element which is common to all of them is raw data.

Why are social networks derived from underlying conversational data significant now?

The reason lies in the popularity of social networks like Facebook and MySpace which have given us many new insights into user behaviour – all of which can be quantified and observed. This means, we can now take a 'retro' approach and apply these new insights from social networks to an existing body of conversational data.

> A data led approach to social media is universal because every organization has access to such data from the many touch points through which it engages with the customer.

However, social relationships are not always explicitly detectable from the user interface; hence it is more important to derive relationships between nodes from the underlying data rather than depend on the information provided by the nodes themselves. For instance, user profiles are often incomplete and are based on easily entered or default information. In contrast, if a relationship can be derived between two nodes based on transactional information, it is more insightful.

A converged data-led approach to social networks applies to many scenarios (from telecom operators, to social networks to airlines) and has many uses ranging from managing trust, combating SPAM, viral propagation of content, managing reputation and social media marketing to name a few.

In this book, we focus on **Social Media Marketing** – which naturally incorporates **Social Media Advertising** also.

> We can take a 'retro' approach; applying new insights from social networks to an existing body of conversational data.

Janus

In any branch of study, creating a unified theory (or a theory of everything[7], to use a Quantum Mechanics terminology), is a complex undertaking. We view the web, telecoms and media holistically. To provide an analogy for our thinking, we use the example of the Roman God Janus, who had the simultaneous ability to look at both the past and the future.

Our first question is: How can we capture the social interactions from the Web, Telecoms and Media in a single concept?

Whatever may be the communication channel a business entity uses data obtained from many touchpoints (social network, media or telecoms) to do two things:

a) Inward-looking – To get new commercial insights about itself (addressing problems like churn reduction/product development etc), or

b) Outward-looking – Addressing how best to acquire new customers (for instance via social media marketing)

---

7   http://en.wikipedia.org/wiki/Theory_of_everything

This data is based on customer conversations obtained from customer touchpoints and not just any raw data (in contrast to a more traditional data warehouse approach).

So, an enterprise has to take a Janus – like approach – inward-looking for some things, such as product development, and outward-looking for others, such as social media campaigns. As we've said, monitoring data and conversations gives us the simultaneous ability to look at both the past and the future.

> Studying data and conversations from various customer touchpoints gives us the ability to take a holistic view – both inside and outside the organization.

Social media marketing – the big picture

What is social media marketing?

> **Social media marketing** is an interaction with a set of online social media conversations from a marketing perspective, based on **converged media** (since conversations can span both technologies and the media).
>
> Social media marketing is measurable via a set of **social media metrics**. These metrics function as the proverbial 'air traffic control' monitoring the domain in **almost real time**. Based on the data driven dials of this interface, the marketer monitors these **many way conversations**.

Ajit Jaokar, Brian Jacobs, Alan Moore and Jouko Ahvenainen

Many-way conversations take place between the marketer and the participants in a social network – but also amongst the participants themselves. The marketer benchmarks the insights gained from these conversations against a set of transactional data (sales, surveys etc) to monitor and tweak a series of **narrowcast (long-tail) campaigns**.

Thus, instead of having one large 'broadcast' campaign – we have many small narrowcast, interactive and ongoing campaigns.

The campaigns and conversations are based on a feedback loop; hence they are iterative and form an ongoing learning experience.

The goals of social media marketing campaigns **include social media advertising, but could also encompass product development, trend monitoring, reducing churn, benchmarking and so on. Specifically, social media marketing can be used as a part of a two stage process: –** first, to identify certain patterns in data, second to verify those observations by specific social media campaigns which also seek **permission** from the customers.

The provider sends personalised messages to the receiver, and over time, the **visibility of the participant's digital footprint grows** and leads to better personalization. Therefore, we start with **passive digital footprints** (based on data patterns) and transition to **active digital footprints** (based on trust).

Our description of **social media marketing** encompasses social media advertising. Social media advertising involves placing advertisements against or within a social media – and it is one activity within the broader field of social media marketing. Parallel to the rise of online social networks and social media marketing, the field of social media analytics is gaining significance. **Social media analytics** is concerned with the measurement and tracking of social media activity. Analytics are important as a currency for advertising, and we discuss them in greater detail below.

Data patterns: the inter-relationship between traditional media, new media and mobility

We are seeing the emergence and convergence of three distinct media types: Mass Media (such as TV or outdoor), Social Media (social networks) and Mobile Media.

Often these media types are discussed in isolation – but they make a lot more sense when viewed holistically in a converged ecosystem constructed from their underlying data patterns.

> Spot the patterns in data usage and validate these patterns using a specific marketing activity over as wide a network as possible (either a converged network or in partnership with a broadcast media channel).

The goal of any commercial media message is to inspire/ persuade the receiver of the message to change the way he or she thinks about a product or service, and ultimately to take a specific action – ideally (but

Ajit Jaokar, Brian Jacobs, Alan Moore and Jouko Ahvenainen

not necessarily) by deciding to purchase something.

'Broadcast media' forms (such as TV, newspapers etc) are often characterized by the belief that they are 'great at building brands'. This is true – as these media forms are indeed best placed to get the advertiser's message across to the widest section of the public. Furthermore, there are very many case-studies that illustrate the relationship between reaching out to lots of people with a suitably well-crafted creative message, and the resultant increase uplift in sales.

It is often said (with some justification) that mass media forms are 'interruptive' in nature; but with an interruptive message, one can generally only know what we already know; there is little scope to learn something new in which we could potentially be interested (direct response data notwithstanding). On the other hand, a message that can be personalised to the recipient involves rather than interrupts and thus could be said to be truly useful. The goal is to work with these two end points (broadcast and interruptive vs. personalised and involving).

Irrespective of how the message is received, ideally the two ends of the media cycle need to co-relate; for every recipient of the message there should be a corresponding action. That action should be tangible and measurable in some way and the advertiser needs to be able to measure how many people received the message and how many of them subsequently took action based on that message.

Traditional media focuses on these two ends of the equation.

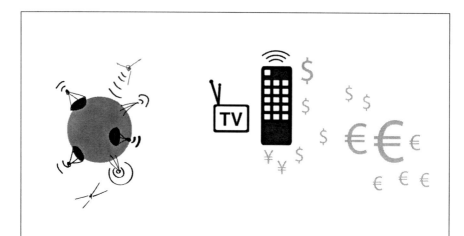

The world of traditional media. In a world of traditional (broadcast) media alone, the message is interruptive and remote control is your only saviour!

Into this mix come social media and mobility – both of which have a unique and a disruptive effect. However, they can also have a synergistic effect when considered together:

The effect of social media is as follows:

The defining characteristic of a social media is its two-way nature. Social media participants are not passive consumers of information or messaging but are also potentially creators of information and messaging; indeed they often have the ability to mutate and evolve all the content that passes through their hands. So, social media can be the reinforcer of the message or the destroyer of the message. Hence, on one hand we get the positive viral effect (the reinforcer) and on the other hand we get the death spiral for the message (the destroyer).

Ajit Jaokar, Brian Jacobs, Alan Moore and Jouko Ahvenainen

The world of social media. In a world of social media, the social media acts to either amplify the message (viral effects) or to shoot it down! Thus, social media can compliment traditional media.

Like the impact of the social media, the impact of mobility is also disruptive for the traditional media. The mobile operator faces a different problem from the broadcaster. The operator might know the customer individually, but not know much about the customer. Specifically, the operator does not know the user's preferences, which can be used to create a more personalised message (and by extension a message that is more likely to be useful to the receiver).

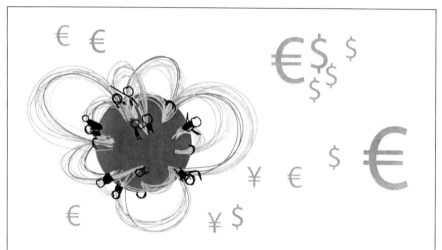

The world of mobile. The world of mobile relates to Patterns, Partnerships and Promotions. The mobile device has the opposite problem from the media company. The operator can identify the customer at an individual level, but does not know the customers preferences, and thus personalisation is limited. Thus we need the three P's – Patterns, Partnerships, Promotions.

Mobile media complements mass media (like television) by providing the individual with the personalization which mass media lacks. This can happen in potentially three interconnected ways:

a) Patterns: Spotting behavioural patterns
b) Promotions: Specific marketing activity or promotions to validate observations from the patterns
c) Partnerships: Creating partnerships between traditional media and mobile media to get as wide a network as possible (or extend your own network within a converged ecosystem)

Patterns: Patterns in usage can be gleaned by merging data streams from outside the telecoms network, along with telecoms data from Call Detail Records. (A Call Detail Record (CDR) is the computer record produced by a telephone exchange containing details of a call that passed through it)

One example of merging data streams could combine program viewing information with CDR's. In this hypothetical example, operators analyse their data alongside program viewing information and discover that at a certain time every week, a group of people on their network communicate via text messages.

If that time coincides with the transmission time of a specific program (say a reality TV show), then potentially these customers are fans of that show and are communicating with each other as they watch the program.

This information can be validated via **promotions** and a specific promotion can be designed to test the hypothesis with an opt-in clause for further communication with the customer.

Finally, a telecoms provider can gain insights if it **partners** with a TV station. Many of these partnerships are already happening with voting via text on TV reality shows. Such a partnership can lead to an opportunity to extend the scope of the network itself beyond mobile, for example by offerings such as fixed network services or IPTV services.

The key is to get a single view of the customer from their data patterns and / or to get an incrementally detailed view of that customer through their social and behavioural interactions (which may need external data sources)and then refine that analysis by specific promotions to validate the observations.

The wider the network (either on its own or in partnership) – the more effective the results. Over time, this process will lead to an understanding of the participant's **digital footprint**.

Social media marketing campaigns are the driver to an increased understanding of the participant's digital footprint through a two stage process. First, to identify certain patterns in data and second to verify those observations by specific social media campaigns which also seek to obtain permission from the customer. In this scenario, the provider is sending personalised messages to the receiver and over time, the visibility of the participant's digital footprint grows and leads to better personalization which adds value for the receiver.

Digital footprints – the foundations of a data driven approach

The idea of digital footprints has increasingly been discussed mainly from a privacy or data protection standpoint. However, it is agreed that we are increasingly leaving larger digital footprints over time, especially given the rise of popular social networks.

A digital footprint is the persistence of data trails online by a user's activity in a digital environment – which **John Battelle** calls the Clickstream exhaust[8].

According to the Pew Internet report[9], there are two main classifications for digital footprints: **Passive Digital Footprints** and **Active Digital Footprints**. A passive digital footprint is created when data is collected about an action without any client activa-

---

8   http://battellemedia.com/archives/000647.php
9   http://www.pewinternet.org/report_display.asp?r=229

tion, whereas active digital footprints are created when a user deliberately releases personal data for the purpose of sharing information about himself.

On the Web, many interactions such as creating a social networking profile, or commenting on a picture in Flickr leaves a digital footprint. In a mobile context, CDRs are the transactional data that constitute the user's digital footprint. But the mere availability of transactional data alone is not enough since privacy and data protection rules will apply to the usage of data (and rightly so!).

There is a paradox with privacy. On one hand everyone fears losing it. Scott McNealy of Sun Microsystems famously said that: consumer privacy is a red herring: we have zero privacy – and we should all get over it[10]. This view has gathered credence after 9/11.

Esther Dyson argues that we need more granular control over our data. She believes that the notion of privacy doesn't fully capture the challenges of the current environment online[11]:"We need to stop talking about privacy and start talking about control over data," she says. She argues that, in the future, users are going to want more granular control over their data, making detailed decisions about what gets shared with whom. "Users may be overwhelmed when first setting up an account, but when they get more comfortable with an application, they will exert more control."

On the other hand, we all have an incentive to contribute data about ourselves, while reflecting on the manner in which we want to be seen, so as to be more visible within a digital context.. For instance, even if

---

10   http://www.wired.com/politics/law/news/1999/01/17538
11   www.pewinternet.org/pdfs/PIP_Digital_Footprints.pdf

you do nothing else except create a profile on LinkedIn[12], you are imme-diately visible on Google. Hence, you are contactable. When you leave a 'digital cookie trace', you create a positive reputation about yourself which is controlled by only you (besides being searchable on the Web). Using the same rationale, we all have a positive incentive to contribute to the Web since it enhances our own reputation and searchability .

> The question for providers is: How do we make the best use of digital footprints to serve the customer, while taking privacy issues into account?

From passive digital footprints to active digital footprints

As discussed earlier , social media marketing campaigns are the driver to an increased understanding of the participant's digital footprint through two stage process of first identifying and then verifying behaviour patterns . The act of verification can take us from the delivery of a generic to a more personalized message. To reiterate, it is important to look at the **interplay between media types (i.e. Web, TV, Mobile and others)** rather than focussing on the developments for a specific media type.

> We start with passive digital footprints (based on behav-ioural data patterns) and transition to active digital foot-prints (based on trust)

---

12   www.linkedin.com

Ajit Jaokar, Brian Jacobs, Alan Moore and Jouko Ahvenainen

We discuss this idea at length below. In the data pattern stage, many customer preferences are 'potential truths', but we can only verify them once we get validations from specific targeted social media campaigns.

For example, we know that the participant could be potentially interested in The Sopranos or Golf and Ferraris based on their behavioural analysis, but we can only verify this from marketing campaigns based on that analysis (a two-stage process which validates information from the available data).

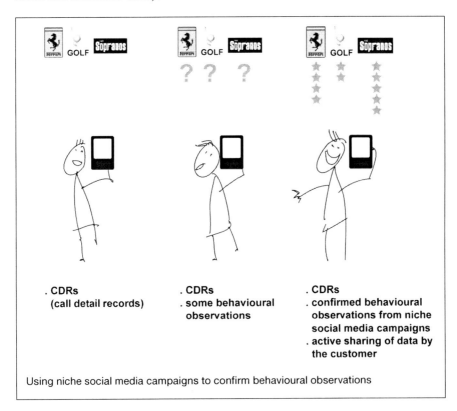

. CDRs
  (call detail records)

. CDRs
. some behavioural
  observations

. CDRs
. confirmed behavioural
  observations from niche
  social media campaigns
. active sharing of data by
  the customer

Using niche social media campaigns to confirm behavioural observations

We thus transition from passive digital footprints to a more trusted, permission-based model of active digital footprints through analysis of behavioural data patterns and social media marketing.

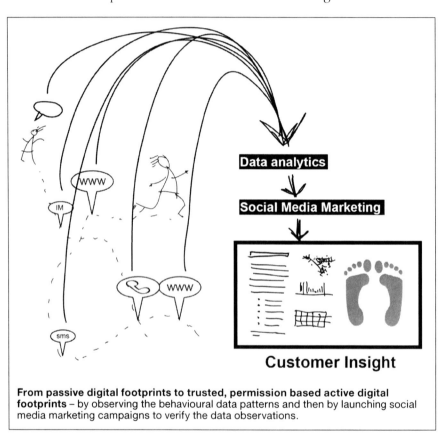

Data analytics

Social Media Marketing

Customer Insight

From passive digital footprints to trusted, permission based active digital footprints – by observing the behavioural data patterns and then by launching social media marketing campaigns to verify the data observations.

Ajit Jaokar, Brian Jacobs, Alan Moore and Jouko Ahvenainen

Social media marketing – A social network perspective

In this section, we view social media marketing from a social network perspective.

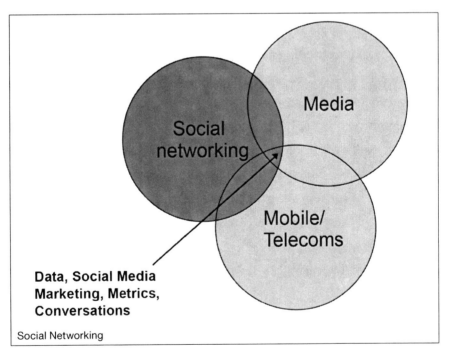

Social Networking

Social networks are becoming increasingly common. They include not only prominent sites like YouTube and Flickr, but also a mechanism for content and information creation (Wikis and Blogs), a mechanism for information and content sharing, such as companycommand.com and noteflight.com and the act of reviewing other people's content (ratings, recommendations, reviews and comments). Underpinning all this peer produced information and content via networked communities are, participants brought together to work on task related goals, that create their own value and not by traditional creators of media content and information

Hot vs. cold media

The change in the media landscape can be described as a transition from 'Cold media' to 'Hot media'. Cold media is interruptive. It lives in a broadcast mode and is built upon the principles of mass media communications, stripping its audience to a model of CPM[13] (*CPM stands for Cost per Mille – Cost per mille , also called cost per thousand (CPT), is a commonly used measurement in advertising*) and other quantitative demographics. It is not built upon passions, desires and individual and collective needs but upon an industrial logic. It is based on the rationale that 'we produce, you consume' and, more importantly, 'we produce at scale, and you consume at scale'. This leads to the logical mindset that: 'We have only one interest in you and that is how much cash we can extract from your wallet'.

But we live increasingly in a digitally interconnected and networked world.

This networked world is the world of the 'hot media'. The concept of hot media involves two-way flow of communication and collaboration

---

13   http://en.wikipedia.org/wiki/Cost_per_mille

that benefits a specific community of interest. As we've already noted, Nokia had forecast in 2008 that by 2012, 25% of all media will be created by us. Thus, we are witnessing the shift to individualised and personalised media consumption, and its creation as a networked practice. Here, a medium of communication is not merely a passive conduit for the transmission of information but rather an active force in creating new social patterns and new perceptual realities. That is the effect of living in a hot media world.

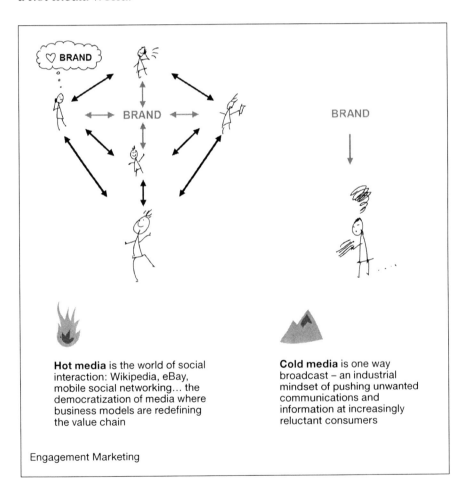

Hot media is the world of social interaction: Wikipedia, eBay, mobile social networking… the democratization of media where business models are redefining the value chain

Cold media is one way broadcast – an industrial mindset of pushing unwanted communications and information at increasingly reluctant consumers

Engagement Marketing

The philosophy behind engagement marketing

Wikipedia describes engagement marketing as:[14]

Engagement marketing, sometimes called "participation marketing," is a marketing strategy that invites and encourages consumers to participate in the evolution of a brand. Rather than looking at consumers as passive receivers of messages, engagement marketers understand that consumers should be actively involved in the production and co-creation of marketing programs. Ultimately, engagement marketing attempts to connect consumers more strongly with brands by "engaging" them in a dialogue and a two-way, cooperative interaction.

People embrace what they create. Hence, the more engaged the community is in co-creating a product or a service, the more likely it is that the final product will be accepted. This idea creates the intellectual foundation behind engagement marketing. For example Lego's co-creation and engagement marketing program underpins everything that the company does.

The world of business, media, and communications is evolving from the straight-lines of an industrial era to the more complex and networked world that mimics the interconnected ecology of nature. This interactive networked world isn't about vertical silos, traditional notions of product and service creation, mass-production and mass media and marketing. It is about the massive flows of people, who are connecting, collaborating, organising and creating in a manner that has nothing to do with a linear approach. As MIT Professor Henry Jenkins outlined in

14 http://en.wikipedia.org/wiki/Engagement_marketing

his book 'Convergence Culture', this is truly an engaged and participatory culture.

For over 150 years, our economies, culture and society have been shaped by a straight-line logic producing considerable economic success. However, with the dawn of the networked-society, a straight-line logic of getting tasks done becomes a barrier to progress.

Why?

This is because, the change wrought by the networked- society is structural – challenging how markets and organisations have co-evolved over the last 150 years, argues Yochai Benkler in the 'Wealth of Networks'.

This creates a dilemma. And the dilemma is :

> How can firms and the people that work in those firms, develop coherent marketing strategies/products and services that are premised upon No-Straight-Line principles when they have been versed only in Straight-Line thinking (at least for people over 35 from birth?

So if the 20th century was about straight-line thinking around commerce, media and communications, the 21st century will be about **Engagement**.

> Indeed if companies spent the 20th century managing efficiencies they will spend the 21st century managing experiences.

The philosophy of Engagement is built upon:

- Accepting the true nature of human beings
- Participation – co-creation- co-innovation- harnessing collective intelligence
- Trust and the transparency of contact
- Context & meaning
- Higher order ideas and beliefs
- Technologies of co-operation
- Understanding how real markets thrive
- Flowability as in information and knowledge flows
  - trust flows – data flows – data analytics – marketing flows
- The role of brands and organisations as being life enabling – life simplifying and navigational
- The Bill Bailey Principle [15] – start with a laugh and work backwards

The philosophy, principles and tools of Engagement could help sell a product, an industry, a region, or be used to combat a social issue. Engagement is about connecting large or small communities to an idea/task/goal/passion that they want to be part of and that they want to share with their friends, driven by a commercial or social agenda.

Engagement Marketing creates stronger customer relationships, greater advocacy and deeper loyalty. If customers are meaningfully engaged with the brand, it is proven to deliver greater value on the business bottom line for multiple stakeholders. It also enables the creation of new business models that make more sense in a participatory culture of no straight lines. Engagement attracts and provides the tools and

---

15   http://www.billbailey.co.uk/

means for communities of affinity to form around issues that are highly motivating to each individual.

The emperor has no clothes
– web 2.0 has no business model

The concept of engagement at an individual level leads to social networking and also to the phenomenon of **Web 2.0**. Like it or not, Web 2.0 has become mainstream. First described in September 2005 in a seminal article by Tim O'Reilly called '**What is Web 2.0**'[16], Web 2.0 has spawned a range of businesses, start-ups and concepts. It is generally deemed to incorporate concepts like user-generated content, 'social' use of the web, 'sharing'/'free' content etc. Yet there is a paradox. Almost three years from the launch of Web 2.0, we now observe a curious phenomenon.

> Web 2.0 was supposed to be funded by advertising yet advertisers do not trust Web 2.0 and social media/user generated content. This paradox illustrates the contradictions between the old world (traditional media) and the new world (social media).

Whatever your definition of Web 2.0 (and there are many), most people will agree that Web 2.0 is mainly based on user-generated content and 'free' services. Hence, because Web 2.0 is supposed to be 'free' in most cases, advertising remains the main revenue model for Web 2.0.

Therein lies the problem, because advertisers do not trust social

---

16 http://oreillynet.com/pub/a/oreilly/tim/news/2005/09/30/what-is-web-20.html

media and user-generated content. We could say that advertisers don't get it – but that would be incorrect since there are hard commercial realities underlying the problem, as we shall discuss below.

If synergies can be found between advertising and the social media, then the whole ecosystem can benefit. On one hand, we could argue that users of social media sites will never accept advertising. But the uptake of Google (and especially Gmail) refutes that argument. Many of us will accept advertising against the most sacrosanct communications (person-to-person email) if that advertising is executed respectfully. So, potentially, the commercial payoffs are huge if we can solve the problem of social media and advertising.

But, first we have to ask ourselves:

> If advertising works for the Web (for example with content search), then why does it not work for the Social Web (with social search)?

Content search vs. social search

For most of us, the touch point to the Web is the **search engine**. But increasingly, we find that many people (especially the young) are using a social network (such as Facebook, MySpace etc) as a starting point for their interaction with the Web.

> We are no longer accessing the Web primarily to search for content, but rather we are accessing the Web to search for and interact with people.

Thus, the **social web / social search** are primarily about searching for and interacting with people.

> Social search differs from content search since it is not possible to tie the query to the Intent.

In other words, when we access the social web, we often do not have a specific intent/purpose since we are often trying to catch up with friends and maybe meet new friends. While the social search can be co-related to content search through **recommendations** or you may buy something because your friend recommends it, but for most part the two are completely different.

Just as content search and content advertising are related, social search and social advertising are related. However, the synergies between social search and social advertising are not very clear. We have already seen what we mean by social search: the search for friends, contacts, business associates etc. Since most social networks are free, it is expected that social networks will be supported by advertising. We refer to advertisements supporting social network activities as **social network advertising** (which is a subset of social network marketing). Advertisers understand content search since it can be tied to an intent, but for reasons we see below, social search (and indeed social media) brings with it a whole new set of challenges and opportunities.

Why advertisers don't like social media

In August 2007, two leading companies (Vodafone and First Direct) chose to pull their advertising from Facebook after they were randomly placed on a Facebook page giving information about a far right party in the UK. [17] This led to considerable uproar and soul-searching in the media (and embarrassment for Vodafone and First Direct). However, at the heart of the problem is a deeper issue. First, the party in question was a legitimate political party even if their views were not consistent with most people's views. Hence, nothing illegal was done here. ***However, the advertisers did not want to associate with the site and here is the most significant element – they had no clue that this would happen and nor did they have a choice.*** The situation arose purely based on how online advertising works: the advertiser buys impressions against a certain site (in this case Facebook). After that, there is limited control as to where exactly within Facebook the advertisements will be displayed.

Which creates a problem.

Social networking sites are different from other sites since the content and the context of the content is not predictable and is dynamic as we have seen in the above example.

The problem gets worse since the context of a conversation is not known. For instance, a Facebook group about Nike[18] may not be flattering to Nike (to take an example the conversation in the group may be about alleged exploitation of child labour by Nike[19]). Hence, it may not be the most appropriate place for Nike to display their advertising. Take another example: if there is a conversation about 'Ford' we don't know if it is about the actor Harrison Ford, the ex-president Gerald Ford[20] or the

---

17 http://www.guardian.co.uk/media/2007/aug/03/farrightpolitics.digitalmedia

18 www.nike.com

19 http://news.bbc.co.uk/1/hi/programmes/panorama/970385.stm

20 http://en.wikipedia.org/wiki/Gerald_Ford

Ford motor company [21]or indeed about Henry Ford[22] the founder of the Ford Motor company.

As Facebook found out much to its dismay with its Beacon program[23] (*Beacon is a part of Facebook's advertisement system that sends data from external websites to Facebook, ostensibly for the purpose of allowing targeted advertisements and allowing users to share their activities with their friends. The privacy issues from Facebook arise because it tracks people individually for the purposes of advertisements.*), advertising on social networks is not easy.

Social networking sites have impressive user numbers: Ning has 267,787 sites, Bebo sees 22 million visitors a month, Club Penguin sees five million visitors per month, LinkedIn gets nearly five million unique visits. Facebook saw 33.9 million unique U.S. visitors in January 2008, and MySpace saw nearly 72 million unique visitors in the same month.

Putting this data in context, 37 million people in the UK currently read a national newspaper every week (source: National Readership Survey, July 07 – June 08).

Despite high valuations, making revenues from these users is a problem for networking sites. Although Facebook is valued at $15 billion dollars, it is still likely to lose money and Google has been unable to monetise its $900 million investment in MySpace[24] . CPMs on social networks are also low. Facebook sets a minimum CPM of $0.15 for its "social ads", and the MySpace banner ad rate stands at a CPM of less than $2. [25]

---

21   www.ford.com

22   http://en.wikipedia.org/wiki/Henry_Ford

23   http://en.wikipedia.org/wiki/Beacon_(Facebook)

24   http://www.alleyinsider.com/2008/2/google_myspace_deal_hurting_us_nws

25   http://www.technologyreview.com/advertisement.aspx?ad=biztech&id=40&redirect=%2FBiztech%2F2092
     2%2F%3Fa%3Df

To quote an article in the MIT technical review,[26] the problem has four facets:

a) **Unsuitable metrics:** CPM may not be the best indicator of social network analysis

b) **Attention (or rather the lack thereof!)**: Members of a social network spend their time in many different activities within the network – thereby fragmenting attention and making advertisements less effective

c) **Privacy:** The reluctance of members of a social network to permit advertisers to access their social transactional data for advertisements (as it had happened with the Facebook Beacon program)

d) **Content:** Not all content in social networks may be appropriate for advertisers to associate their brands with.

So, what can be done to alleviate this problem?

Peter Drucker[27], widely regarded as the father of modern management, once said:'*What gets measured gets managed*'[28].

Between the eras of Web 1.0(1999/2000) to Web 2.0 (2005 onwards), the advertising model on the Web has reached maturity. However, the advertising model on the social web (social networks) is far from accepted. One of the reasons for this is the lack of relevant metrics

---

26 http://www.technologyreview.com/advertisement.aspx?ad=biztech&id=40&redirect=%2FBiztech%2F2092 2%2F%3Fa%3Df

27 http://en.wikipedia.org/wiki/Peter_Drucker

28 http://www.thinkarete.com/quotes/by_teacher/Peter%20Drucker

---

Ajit Jaokar, Brian Jacobs, Alan Moore and Jouko Ahvenainen

(measurements) since existing metrics like CPM[29] do not apply to social networks.

A second issue is appropriateness; advertisers can engage with users via social network sites but they need to do so within the conventions of the medium. These conventions are not the same as those which exist within more traditional media forms, where something of a pact exists between the user and the advertiser. The user accepts that to get free stuff (like commercial TV broadcasts) he or she needs to tolerate advertiser messages. This contract, or pact, does not exist within social media forms, which in themselves are much more analogous to a conversation between friends. Advertisers don't always understand this convention and thus their messages are not tolerated – indeed they are often resented.

To gain acceptance, advertisers need to 'fit' within the medium (cynics may say that this has always been the case in traditional media also – and they would be correct) but within social media the big difference is that the advertiser is very clearly not in control not only of receptivity but also of subsequent action concerning what is done with his message. After all, if an ad on TV or in a newspaper doesn't 'fit' or isn't appropriate to the individual reader/viewer it's ignored. The advertiser may or may not know the extent of this 'ignoring' and anyway he can argue that all advertising has an effect, however subliminally, and that there is no such thing as bad publicity. Within social media sites simply ignoring something because it is inappropriate is less common; making your displeasure felt because of the inappropriateness of the advertiser's message is far more common. There is most certainly such a thing as bad

---

29   http://en.wikipedia.org/wiki/Cost_per_mille

publicity on the Internet.

Thus, the issue of lack of control is a major one from the advertiser's standpoint.

In the old model advertisers controlled messaging. They decided what was said and where. Now there is anarchy! Users decide on what is said, ideas spin off all over the place and marketers aren't in control. Metrics help to some extent by providing a balance and a measure of influence.

Social networks and metrics go well together because the mathematical theories underlying social networks have existed for a long time.

So what's changed?

What has changed is the availability of data in a digital format through online social networks, which makes social relationships navigable.

Social relationships can be mapped using a technique called the Graph Theory. The principles underlying social networks and the Graph Theory[30] have been with us since 1736 following a paper written by Leonhard Euler[31] on the Seven Bridges of Königsberg[32]. Terms like 'social graph' and six degrees of separation are now entering our vocabulary (there was a Broadway play and subsequently a movie called 'Six Degrees of Separation'[33].)

However, while the social graph and its applications are now becoming significant because of the emergence of Web-based social net-

---

30   http://en.wikipedia.org/wiki/Graph_theory
31   http://en.wikipedia.org/wiki/Leonhard_Euler
32   http://en.wikipedia.org/wiki/Seven_Bridges_of_K%C3%B6nigsberg
33   http://en.wikipedia.org/wiki/Six_Degrees_of_Separation_(film)

Ajit Jaokar, Brian Jacobs, Alan Moore and Jouko Ahvenainen

works, *the application of the advertising model to social networks remains a missing link – the solution to which is commercially very significant especially if it is quantifiable through metrics that can be easily understood by everyone within the industry.*

From the age of mass media to an age of networks

As we have seen in the previous sections, we are transitioning from mass media to social media dominated by social networks. In this context, we use the term **mass media** to define traditional media and use a definition adapted from the book 'The Network Society' [34]by Jan van Dijk [35]. Jan van Dijk characterises a mass media society as being based on the concept of large collectives and is shaped by homogenous groups, organizations and communities ('masses') often organized in a physical co-presence. Mass media society is characterised by the media and communication technologies of the fifties and the sixties in western countries. We contrast mass media societies to a network society.

In a mass media society, the basic units are the large collective 'masses'. In contrast, a network society is based on individuals who form voluntary connections with other individuals regardless of location. In a network society, the network becomes a basic unit of organization at all levels (individuals, groups and organizations). Online social networks, media networks and technology networks act as the catalysts for a networked society.

Society today is in a state of transition from being predominantly mass media to network dominated. Increasingly, the networked society

---

34   http://www.gw.utwente.nl/vandijk/
35   http://en.wikipedia.org/wiki/Jan_van_Dijk

is becoming the dominant format. Both mass media and networks will co-exist but the question is: *What happens when the networked society becomes the dominant form of organization?*

The term 'network society'[36] is jointly attributed to two researchers – Manuel Castells[37] and Jan van Dijk[38]. Manuel Castells believes that networks have become the basic unit of modern society. Jan van Dijk differs slightly from Castells in that he believes that modern society still consists of individuals, groups and organizations, though increasingly they are being organized and linked in social and social media networks[39]. We draw on both these definitions in this book and address the question*: If networks become the basic building blocks of the society – what is the impact on media and communications?*

Some of these changes are obvious. Propelled by digitization, networks are increasingly impacting traditional media and we are already living with these changes. As media becomes digitized, it transcends formats. It also becomes interactive as consumers become creators. At this point, mechanisms like region-coded DVDs[40] do not work very well. Business models change as well; for instance the same clip/video can not only be seen on a DVD but also on YouTube. How should such media be monetized?

Advertising seems to be the logical answer. Indeed, in the book 'Crossing the Chasm'[41], Geoffrey Moore defines a market[42] as:

---

36 http://en.wikipedia.org/wiki/Network_society
37 http://en.wikipedia.org/wiki/Manuel_Castells
38 http://en.wikipedia.org/wiki/Jan_van_Dijk
39 http://www.gw.utwente.nl/vandijk/research/network_theory/network_theory_plaatje/a_theory_outline_outline_of_a.doc/
40 http://en.wikipedia.org/wiki/DVD_region_code
41 http://en.wikipedia.org/wiki/Crossing_the_Chasm
42 http://www.parkerhill.com/Summary%20of%20Crossing%20the%20Chasm.pdf

---

- A set of actual or potential customers
- For a given set of products or services
- Who have a common set of needs or wants, and
- *Who reference each other when making a buying decision* (*emphasis the authors'*)

Hence, because a social network fulfils the above criteria (especially the ability to reference customers), a social network can act as a foundation for a market provided its unique limitations can be overcome. However, due to its data-driven characteristic, social media advertising is a lot like prospecting for gold as opposed to building a cathedral.

To understand this point, we have to appreciate the unique characteristics of social media and its data driven nature. Mass media is driven by demand. Social media is driven by supply. Creating a mass media venture (for instance a newspaper) is like building a cathedral. You need a plan and you need to anticipate demand first. In contrast, a social media venture originates from the concept of supply. Demand is not anticipated in advance. Hence, social media advertising is a lot like prospecting for gold where you sieve through volumes of silt (data) in order to get to the nuggets of gold (the salient facts that unlock the advertising revenue).

One problem facing companies that want to present a commercial message within a social network context, is that their inventory is currently limited to formats that were created many, years ago. In a search, or pull economy, currency or value is based upon relevant information. So perhaps the furniture of advertising needs to change?

We explain the concept of cathedral vs. prospecting in greater detail below since it is the heart of our data-driven approach.

To recap, mass media was driven by demand and social media is driven by supply. We explain this concept by studying the death of a newspaper, an example of old media in crisis. We use a newspaper since it is globally understood as a media format. The example is based on a similar one from the book 'Mobile Web 2.0' by Ajit Jaokar and Tony Fish[43].

We can summarise per the diagram below. Mass media is based on the idea of silos of media formats (radio, TV, newspapers etc) and one-way conversations (the customers are passive consumers). Social media on the other hand is based on the idea of many grass root conversations which are filtered and refined by the community. Hence mass media starts with a clear purpose in mind and a definite format. Social media on the other hand is emergent and starts off as a conversation.

> These conversations lead to a high volume of data – and consequently the need to prospect for gold, or patterns, relationships, alpha users etc upon which the idea of social media advertising is based.

---

43   www.mobileweb20.futuretext.com

Ajit Jaokar, Brian Jacobs, Alan Moore and Jouko Ahvenainen

Mass media in a death spiral – lessons from the newspaper industry

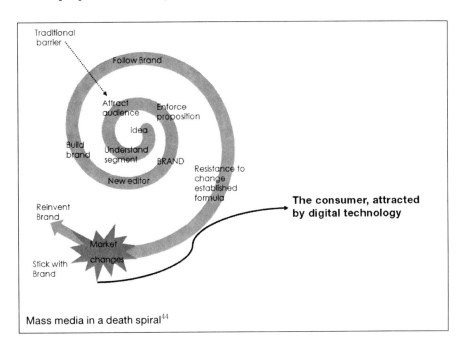

Mass media in a death spiral[44]

Let us look at the genesis and evolution of the newspaper industry to illustrate the impact of social media on traditional media. Most of today's established newspapers were started between a hundred and two hundred and fifty years ago.

The idea for a new newspaper generally originated with a proprietor whose main driver was the pursuit of power and influence. He hired an editor, whose responsibility was to create content and an opinion that fitted the vision of the proprietor. Whilst the editor was not the owner of the vision, he would certainly agree with the direction and was more than

---

44   www.amfventures.com

capable of translating the proprietor's vision into words and pictures.

The business model was a mix of the cover price paid by the buyer and advertising. As more people bought the newspaper, the charges for advertising in the paper went up , and the cover-price revenue increased.

Assuming that the newspaper became successful, the proprietor and his editor had now created a media property or a brand. Over time the editor moved on, or was moved on, and a new editor was selected for his/her insight and understanding of the readership (and of the proprietor's vision).

The new editor's role was to build the brand further, hopefully by maintaining its values, and thus its reader base. The new editor rarely was in a position to 'rock the boat' – rather he/she reinforced the original proposition. As new editors came and went, slowly, 'passion' was replaced by 'building the brand' or conforming to the 'house style'.

Assuming that the title's values continued to reflect the values of a sufficiently large number of people, and assuming that the production process was efficiently managed, the publication made money. This cosy relationship between the newspaper and its readership continued until the rise of the Web when it changed forever.

The rise and success of the Web meant that the consumer became the creator. The traditional barriers to entry; large numbers of correspondents, cost of paper and production, and marketing migrated if not to zero, then certainly in that direction.

Everyone interested in a topic became empowered and was thus able(should they choose to do so) to take on the role of a creator. The community as a whole took on the role of an editor. At first, newspapers (and other traditional media forms) ignored the threat of user-generated content but when advertising dollars began to migrate to newer online properties and communities such as MySpace the industry was hit hard, and reacted by migrating their own content online, following the old maxim that 'if you can't beat them, join them'.

This migration has not been unsuccessful; as can be illustrated by the numbers. 'The Guardian' (www.guardian.co.uk) achieved almost 26 million unique users in one month, averaging at 1.379 million unique users per day in October 2008 (source: ABCe). Similar migrations by 'The Telegraph Group' and 'The Times have' delivered similar numbers, and have led Rupert Murdoch of News Corporation to make the point that 'newspapers' have become 'news brands'.

The success of sites like The Guardian's suggest that there is certainly a role for an editor. This is easy to explain. As the sheer volume of available content grows, there is a need to select the good from the bad. On sites without professional editorial support, the community is in theory able to step in to perform the function of the editor (the filter) by commenting, tagging, rating and so on. Examples of such sites include: Digg and YouTube. Social media follows a completely different pattern from newspapers. There is often no 'plan'. A blog is started by an individual since the barriers to entry are so low. In many cases, the individual has no defined end-reader or customer in mind. The blog grows and evolves. It starts to be referenced by others. Most importantly, many such blogs emerge, even if by far and away the majority (some have estimated over 90%) then fall into non-use and become in effect defunct.

In contrast, due to the barriers implicit in the cost of print and infrastructure few newspapers are started.

There are exceptions that illustrate how these barriers can be overcome. Sharing print resources, scraping information and stories from the likes of the Press Association and the Web (ironically), as opposed to, in-house journalists, reducing the cost to the reader to zero, and satisfying a consumer need for something to read on a crowded commuter journey has led to the advertising-funded success of free newspapers like Metro.

Metro's (and other free newspapers') reliance on the Web as a source of information; the use by journalists of social media sites as sources for follow-ups to stories (how much easier it is to trace someone via these sites than by going door-to-door); and the emergence of newspaper sites as satisfying a real consumer need for 24 hour news and information are all examples of the co-existence of the old with the new.

In the next section, we will see social media marketing from the perspective of a traditional media company.

Social media marketing: A media perspective

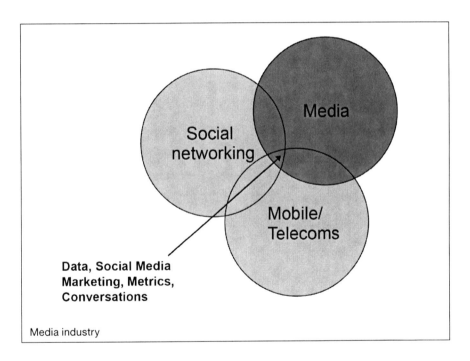

Introduction

In the previous section, we saw the impact of social media on the newspaper medium. In this section, we will explore the growth of social media from the perspective of traditional media.

We define traditional media to include media types that are predominantly broadcast; in other words, those media forms that send a message to a consumer, and whose relationship with that consumer is as a receiver of that message, as opposed to a creator of content.

Broadly, this includes media types that existed before the Web like **TV, radio, newspapers, magazines, cinema and out-of-home advertising**. These traditional media are also evolving (see the example above on how newspapers are both moving content online, and are taking content from online) and many of them now include some form of interactivity. For example the partnership between Satellite-TV firm Dish Network and ad-tech firm Invidi claims to target advertising and dynamic commercial insertion based on factors like location. Within mainstream TV broadcasting, SMS based voting on reality shows is now common place all over the world.

Extending the example of the Guardian newspaper from the last section further, it's worth remembering that no single media form has ever led to the demise of another. TV didn't kill radio in the US; video and (later) DVD players did not kill cinema; personal video recorders (PVR's) are yet to kill TV, and so on. Indeed TV continues to thrive in spite of (indeed as we shall see, alongside) the Internet. Traditional media forms evolve and adapt. Newspapers and TV go online and use online media forms to complement what they do in traditional media.

A great example of the complementarity of media forms came in the recent US election. Much was made of **Barack Obama's** use of all forms of digital media, which was indeed spectacularly successful, but it's worth remembering that he also bought far more TV airtime that his rival, including 30 minutes worth in an infomercial-style message that went a long way to putting the final nail into the McCain

Ajit Jaokar, Brian Jacobs, Alan Moore and Jouko Ahvenainen

campaign. Obama spent a measured $640 million on campaigning versus John McCain's $360 million; and on TV alone outspent his rival by $80 million. As one UK sage, Jeremy Bullmore, commented in 'Campaign' magazine when asked to speculate on how all of this media activity had helped sway the result: 'Money, good. More money, better'.

Newspapers had a role to play too. On the day of the election, 270,000 copies of the Chicago Tribune were sold – as against a regular circulation of c. 50,000. One local paper was even selling copies on eBay!

The point is that, media evolves; media forms have their own strengths; consumers use them for different things, at different times, to match different moods.

We have seen before that traditional media like TV is ideally placed for building awareness. But these media forms are used by advertisers for other things than simply reaching the mass market – including changing or reinforcing image, perception and consumer attitudes. Hence, FMCG[45](Fast moving consumer goods) categories like toiletries, soap, detergents, product categories like cars and financial services, and brands like Volkswagen, Lloyds TSB, Dove, Ariel and Coca-Cola continue to spend large amounts on traditional media.

Thus, traditional and new media forms co-exist today and will in our opinion continue to co-exist for many years to come. Indeed, there are many instances when traditional media will be still the primary form of content consumption. For instance, during the 2002 soccer World Cup in Japan and Korea, many analysts thought (incorrectly as it turned out) that because of the time difference between Korea/Japan and the rest of the world, more people would watch these tournaments on their lap-

45   http://en.wikipedia.org/wiki/Fast_moving_consumer_goods

tops or portable devices. The fact was that many people continued to watch the matches on the big screen with their friends in the pub, in their offices (many of which opened early). We see that this trend of co-existence will continue.

The media industry value chain

The media industry is mature and complex – and as we see below, it will evolve even more in the near future.

The media industry value chain is driven by the **advertiser** (say Nike or Coke) who essentially pays the dollars. The brand approaches the **media agency**. From the perspective of the agency, their role is to mix and match the different media types to meet the defined needs of the client. So, the newer media types like the Web, Mobile and now social networks are all a part of the **'media mix'** from a media agency's point of view. Note also, for the purposes of our discussion, we are using the term 'the agency' as a unified entity; in reality there are more likely to be separate business entities that fulfil the role of 'the agency' as described below.

The agency has three core roles of relevance to this discussion (we stress 'core'; clearly there are other functions):

a) **Creative function**: Creating the actual ideas and concepts for the advertisements

b) **Communications planning function**: Deciding the choice of media channels to be used and how the budget will be split between them

c) **Media buying function**: Buying the or time in specific TV airtime, radio, print, Web (etc) vehicles. The web sites are often referred to as publishers. These publishers may be accessed directly but more often are bought and sold through aggregators.

 Ajit Jaokar, Brian Jacobs, Alan Moore and Jouko Ahvenainen

When it comes to the Web (or the digital world in general), there are some additional options for the brand. In addition to accessing Web properties via media agencies, brands can also go directly to **advertisement exchange sites** such as Google/Doubleclick, or they could go through **specialist networks** like GLAM media – a network focussed primarily on the female demographic[46] and FM publishing – a network focussed on high traffic thought leader sites[47] and others. This evolution is depicted in the diagram below.

The advertisement exchange and the specialist network space are evolving very fast and are largely independent of the traditional media agency function. While a media agency could indeed approach these networks to place advertisements on behalf of their clients as part of a marketing mix, many of the advertisement exchanges and specialist networks have their own 'Client ad sales function' or often a 'Self service function' where clients are encouraged to place advertisements directly on to their media properties. This is a rapidly growing segment.

This segment is well placed to give precise, reliable feedback in terms of media metrics to the client based on their direct relationship to the media properties (for example web sites in their networks), which a traditional media agency finds harder to do (if they do not own a media network or an ad network). Today, this trend also extends to mobile networks like **Flirtomatic**[48], **itsmy.com**[49] and others. It also leads to the logical creation of full-service sales organisations that are oriented to the

---

46 www.glammedia.com
47 www.federatedmedia.net
48 www.flirtomatic.com
49 www.itsmy.com

digital/mobile space like **Admob**[50] or the **Nokia Ad service**[51]. All these newer players are full fledged digital outlets providing a one stop shop for the brand via a direct sales force.

Traditional media owners have always generated a proportion of their revenue direct from the advertisers (as opposed to via the advertiser's agency), so in one sense this development is nothing new. But given the sheer volume of web sites, the close relationship between content and commercial message, and the opportunity for fast feedback of metrics, this method of direct selling is well-suited to the digital space.

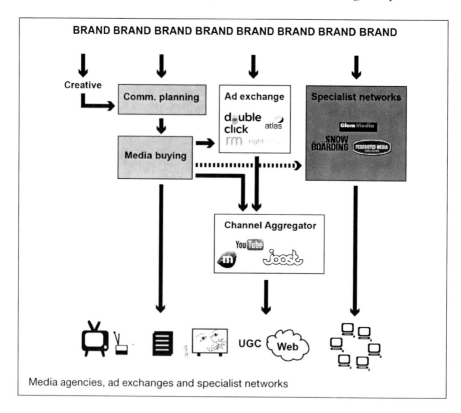

Media agencies, ad exchanges and specialist networks

---

50   www.admob.com

51   http://www.advertising.nokia.com/

Publishers are the owners of the media. In earlier days they were just this – people who published printed material (magazines, newspapers etc). Today we could use the expression media owners as it encompasses broadcasters, outdoor vendors, internet site owners and so on. Also, today's publishers are often consumers – they're the ones delivering the content, by publishing material online.

Money flows from the brand owner to the brand management team to the media agency and to media owner (notwithstanding our comment above on direct sales). Most brand managers will give the media and creative agency budget. The output expected from the first is a plan (how to spend the budget); from the second it's an idea and an end piece of communication.

The media agency's plan is data driven; the planner needs to answer the questions: 'who', when', 'where' in order to get to a plan that will deliver a return on investment to his client. Once the plan is approved, the agency sets about buying (spending the money basically). Then they report back on what was achieved against the plan, and what was achieved in terms of ROI. Learnings are formalised, and fed back into the next planning cycle. This process has evolved over time. It is a common misconception that today's media agencies are simply buyers, and furthermore that they are only interested in TV. In fact the media agencies of today have a strong claim to be true communications advisers, working within what is often described as a 'media neutral' framework.

The term 'media neutral' is a rather neat expression that summarises how things have changed.

In the 'old' full-service agency days, creative people would be briefed by the client, and would subsequently come up with an idea, which would lead to an ad. Let's assume this was a TV ad (as it very often was). The media department of the agency would then prepare a detailed rationale for the client on why the campaign recommendation was to use TV (as opposed to radio or outdoor, for instance). The truth was rather simpler than the analyses contained in these recommendations – the creative team had often already come up with a TV ad, so placing it anywhere else other than on TV wouldn't make a whole lot of sense!

> In a nutshell, in the earlier days, the creatives would work out what to say, and then the media guys would justify where to say it.

Today's media agencies are working within a much more complicated and extensive media world – and one in which the client has more options. This means that they need to start from a different point instead of starting off with a piece of advertising that will only work on one medium. They need to consider:

- Who to talk to, or (perhaps more pertinently) with?
- When to talk to/with them?
- What environment or context to talk to/with them in?
- What mindset they want the receiver to be in when he/she receives the message or engages in the dialogue?

Only then do they try to move on to what to say to those with whom they wish to communicate. 'media neutral' means everyone starts with no preconceptions as to the most appropriate and effective choice of communication channels, or the most appropriate and effective way of using those channels.

In other words, in today's world, the message follows the medium.

The communication planning function becomes a vital skill in which today's media agencies are experts. **Understanding, defining and quantifying the make-up of the most valuable group of people to reach out to them with messaging across platforms (i.e. across media channels) becomes fundamental.**

The media agency's need for data and audience metrics stretches beyond the number of people, and the number of times they will be exposed to the message (which are measured by audience surveys). Today's agencies look to go far beyond these exposure metrics (although of course these still remain important) to consider the frame of mind of the receivers of these messages and also understand how that mind-state can be changed by external and internal influences, and be impacted by the different contexts within which the message is placed.

> The remit for media agencies now stretches 'beyond expo-sure metrics' to consider the frame of mind of the receivers of these messages and also understand how that mind-state can be changed by external and internal influences, and be impacted by the different contexts within which the message is placed.

The one essential that has not changed is the need for data. As we have said, media data used to be about exposure, and a currency for buying and selling. Today, data is what fuels the media agencies'thinking and planning, not just their buying. Data leads to insights and ideas – but insights and ideas based on and rooted in consumer behaviour. This point is critical in considering how media agencies take account of, and plan activity in social media forms.

> Data leads to insights and ideas – but insights and ideas based on and rooted in consumer behaviour

An agency's work typically starts with a set of objectives and briefs. Classically, there will be a business objective (introduce a new line, improve profits, sell more volume, whatever the defined need) and a set of action plans to set against each. Out of each business objective will emerge a marketing objective, and a set of actions. Out of each marketing objective a communication objective, and set of actions. The media agency enters, typically, at the marketing objective stage, and is closely involved in the setting of communication objectives and actions. The agency's first major task is to write the plan.

This **plan** is in effect a concise recommendation of how different communication channels are to be used to meet the set objectives. The agency needs to balance the channels – how much of one, how little of another – based on how each delivers against the criteria outlined above (who, when, where, mind-state, context and so on). At this stage, the issue is which channels to use as opposed to which specific vehicles to use – for example, is there a role for mobile, or for social media, or for TV?

Ajit Jaokar, Brian Jacobs, Alan Moore and Jouko Ahvenainen

Any plan involves the agency making a number of choices – and these choices are driven by data. Take the issue of the target market. Who, or which group represents the group most likely to lead to a return on the client's investment? This might be non-users of the brand (if the marketing objective is to bring new users into the brand), or those who are most loyal to the brand (if the objective is to upsell new services to them).

Diagrammatically, a simplified process flow is illustrated below; with the 'dashed' arrows representing the 'old' way of doing things, using proxies (like simple demographics) in place of the real marketing target; and the normal arrows the more efficient, more targeted route that is often possible today, assuming the data exists.

In this example, the planner will note the importance of peer opinion. This might lead him towards social media forms. But this may not be correct. How does he know that the consumers of greatest interest and relevance to him are users of social media sites? They may just talk face-to-face with their friends and families. And, if they do use social media forms, which forms? Telephony? Online sites? And, if they do use online sites, which sites, when and how often?

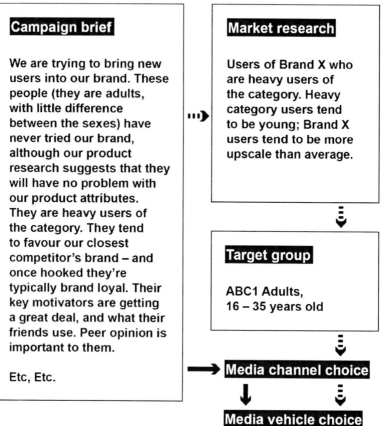

Campaign brief

We are trying to bring new users into our brand. These people (they are adults, with little difference between the sexes) have never tried our brand, although our product research suggests that they will have no problem with our product attributes. They are heavy users of the category. They tend to favour our closest competitor's brand – and once hooked they're typically brand loyal. Their key motivators are getting a great deal, and what their friends use. Peer opinion is important to them.

Etc, Etc.

Market research

Users of Brand X who are heavy users of the category. Heavy category users tend to be young; Brand X users tend to be more upscale than average.

Target group

ABC1 Adults, 16 – 35 years old

Media channel choice

Media vehicle choice

Changing operations of media agencies

The key to making sense of all of this is data; data to help the planner choose the most appropriate media mix; data to sort out the hierarchy of media forms – which are the most significant, relevant and important, which are most likely to generate the greatest return-on-investment? Data to select the individual vehicles to carry the message.

Understanding **how many**, **how** and **when** consumers consume communication channels has always been the key to good planning.

Adding to this an understanding of **why** consumers consume the channels they do, and the **likely consequences** of their actions adds a dimension and improves the plan.

Good data is at the start, and at the heart of this process. From data flows insight; from insight emerges creativity; from creativity come results, measured and evaluated though data. We extend this idea (the importance of measurement) in the next section.

The importance of measurement

We have seen in the last section that media planning and buying has always relied on measurement. Traditional media has been driven by Sarnoff's law, which states that the value of a broadcast network is dependent on the size of the network[52] or the audience. Since David Sarnoff (who created this law) came from a radio industry background, this law applied to the scenario as it existed in the early 1930s. From the customer's perspective, the media industry's emphasis on reach and audience size has led to a famous quote attributed to both Lord Leverhume and John Wanamaker[53]: *"Half the money I spend on advertising is wasted. The trouble is, I do not know which half." Having said that, and perhaps because of that very criticism, traditional media has always invested heavily in measurement.*

In the UK, much of this investment has been via the JICs – the Joint Industry Committees. JICs – for example JICNARS for the national press and magazines, JICREG for the regional press[54], BARB (which used to be called JICTAR) for TV; JICRAR for radio; and POSTAR for out-of-home.

---

52   http://en.wikipedia.org/wiki/Sarnoff's_law
53   http://en.wikipedia.org/wiki/John_Wanamaker
54   http://www.jicreg.co.uk/

Each JIC uses a measurement technique specific and appropriate for the medium. In the case of TV, the BARB system measures audience size and make up via a set-top box and a push-button key-pad placed in a panel of homes across the UK. This approach provides a currency for trading, the buying and selling of airtime, based around the levels of exposure achieved by different time slots and programmes on the medium. In the case of press, an interview is used to arrive at a measure of average issue readership. In radio, a self-completion diary is used. In every case, basic currency information is collected and used for the buying and selling of space and time.

In the USA the commissioning system is different (formal JICs are seen as undesirable) although many of the techniques are similar. Here research companies take the lead – companies like AC Nielsen for TV, and Arbitron for radio.

Currency information on the web is from companies like Comscore. It is now possible to measure social media exposure (example from blog-osphere) from sites like Cymfony[55]

All the above are largely about the exposure data needed to buy and sell space – and as such they are very largely the province of the media buyer and his sales counterpart.

As we've seen above, planners need far more specific and focused consumer data, some of which comes from industry-available surveys such as The Target Group Index (TGI) and (in the UK) the IPA Touch-points study.

But the majority of agencies' planning insights come from client or issue-specific, or agency-proprietary surveys, some of which are panel

---

[55] http://www.cymfony.com/

based, whilst others are more ad hoc in nature. Agencies also regularly commission focus groups in order to gain qualitative insights into how and why consumers behave the way that they do.

Measurement notwithstanding, advertising dollars continue to migrate to the Web; this trend will increase over time as consumers' consumption of traditional media like newspapers and even television continue to reduce as they spend more time online.

> "One statistic we can quote with certainty is that GroupM will invest at least \$4bn for our clients (in all forms of digital interactive media) in 2008, a 75% increase on 2007 in constant currency."
>
> Source: GroupM 'Interaction 2008'

Despite the efforts of players like some UK national newspapers and commercial broadcasters, many traditional media owners have continued to be slow in their adoption of new techniques and approaches relevant to the new world of media interactivity. Historically, the strongest players in one format have not been the leading players in a newer format. The same is true of the Web and traditional media.

The main advertising focus in the dotcom era was the way in which media agencies and their advertisers used the Web as 'just another channel' to reach consumers. Because of the user backlash against banner advertising, pop-ups and the like, this approach never took off. With social media and the increasing use of the Web to create, rather than to consume, content, the participants (who as we have seen are no longer mere consumers) play an increasingly dominant role. This trend will continue. Older and newer forms of media will coexist but the traditional media (and the agencies and the advertisers they serve) will need to find their niche in the new world – a world in which user-generated content plays an important part.

> Today's moms are living in 'double time' averaging a 27 hour waking day. Eight of these hours are spent using media, mainly for parenting advice and tips, led by the internet at 2.6 hours per day."
>
> Source: OMD

The shift in the competitive landscape and the rise of new entrants

As we have indicated before, the Web and social media have led to a fundamental shift in the landscape, due in large part to the rise of new players on the Web who control the entire value chain. Some social media networks now have the ability to provide a 'one stop shop' to the advertiser by including the sales engine, sales team, Web properties and evaluative metrics as a part of its offerings.

As we've seen, brands themselves have a choice. They can go directly to the Web players (for example specialist networks focussed on specific demographics) rather than to a media, or advertising agency. The rise of Google (Adserve/Adsense) has also raised the bar for advertising due to the pay-per-click model. These developments led Sir Martin Sorrell of WPP famously to describe Google as a 'Frenemy'; on one hand his media agencies need to do business with them (as 'friends'), on the other hand they are a threat to future revenue (or, 'the enemy').

Historically, media agency planners have struggled to justify the inclusion of social media channels in their plans. This has less to do with the fact that they feel the need to treat social media like any other channel (talk to any media planner and he or she will always speak at length about the growing importance of this form of communication, and the different rules that apply), and more to do with a lack of reliable, relevant, objective metrics to allow them to quantify and thus justify the medium.

It is also the case that social media forms need, in fact demand, a different creative approach (more subtle, more integrated, less 'advertising') to that employed within most other channels. And many media agency planners are uncomfortable with challenging creative approaches.

> "Amongst blog writers, 28% share opinions on products and brands." Source: Universal McCann

Consequently, major publishers are attempting to move up the value chain by evolving their own (often self service) advertising portals where brands can advertise against specific sites. Ad networks are becoming ad exchanges by providing a self-service function. There are some large players in this space already like Google-DoubleClick, Yahoo-Rightmedia, and Microsoft-Atlas. These entities are essentially Web (or technology) players like Google, Yahoo and Microsoft acquiring companies that served media agencies (like DoubleClick). Even publishers with multiple sites are starting to create their own advertisement sales operations. User-generated content and mobile are viewed as key emerging sectors within a world that is changing and mutating very quickly.

Gaps and opportunities

Having taken a holistic view of both the media and the social networking landscape, we see the following gaps which are yet to be addressed by the industry – and this book hopes to go some way towards starting a discussion around these questions:

a) Collaborative community peer production and participatory user-generated content is a key growth area for the Web – but we do not see any metrics in that space. As we've seen, metrics are key in the generation of revenue.

b) The media agencies will continue to be significant. While we see that many brands will work with digital ad networks, the role of the agency in providing an objective, holistic, single point of contact for a brand across all media forms – will remain. In that role, an agency does not have a way to buy exposures within social media forms, and furthermore struggles to measure the return on the investment in this medium. Again, metrics are key.

c) At the moment, there is no real and meaningful link between observing how people actually behave (via data) and how they feel, or say they will behave (via market research). These are complimentary aspects of marketing, and yet they often exist in silos. Much research spend could be saved if existing customer data were properly explored; and many marketing dollars could be saved if all targeting avenues were examined by understanding (or even better predicting) customer behaviour.

We explore these ideas in the following sections.

Ajit Jaokar, Brian Jacobs, Alan Moore and Jouko Ahvenainen

Social media marketing: A telecoms perspective

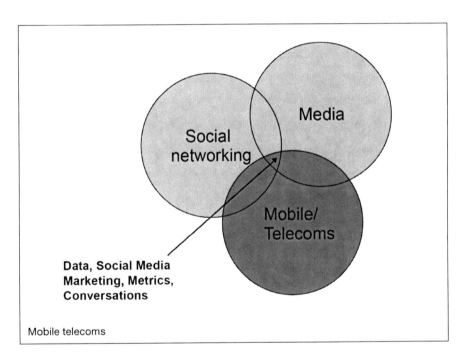

Mobile telecoms

Owning the customer – vs. knowing the customer

Having looked at the social networking and media perspective, we now address the telecoms / mobile perspective. Telecoms/mobile is the newest entrant to this space and going forward, telecoms and mobile networks will grow in importance because of the amount of data a telecoms network captures. If Google's goal is to organise the world's information (Sergey Brin)[56] – then the telecom industry already has large amounts of that information flowing through its networks. In addition, the mobile device is a key element of the digital footprint since it is oriented towards capturing information (which is a driver of the digital footprint). The real question for the telecoms/mobile industry is what can they do with all this information? More importantly, what could they do in the future with all this information?

> If Google's goal is to organise the world's information (Sergey Brin)[57] – then the telecom industry already has large amounts of that information flowing through its networks.

While some telecoms and mobile networks understand the full potential of data, many are only now addressing the issue. In addition, telecoms network operators persist in the quaint notion of **owning the customer**. This obsession causes a blind spot because they miss out on the opportunities of **knowing the customer**. While Operators continue to try to 'own' the customer – the web players continue to 'know' the customer better. Since most people will want to centralize their personal information with a few players, the longer the telecoms industry delays knowing the customer, the more they will lose out. This fact makes it all the more imperative that telecoms and mobile networks address the issue of social networks, socially networked media, social media marketing and the implications for networks.

The familiar argument goes, we (telecoms) have a lot of details

56 http://www.computerweekly.com/Home/tags/sergey-brin.htm
57 http://www.computerweekly.com/Home/tags/sergey-brin.htm

about our customers, due to the transactional information in Call Detail Records (CDRs[58]), we can tell you a lot about the customer.

But, so can a bank!

And if a bank attempts to 'bundle' insurance every time we book a flight on the web through a bank card. Most people will (rightly) be annoyed and sue them for lack of privacy.

So, the notion of customer intimacy on the basis of call data records alone is ambitious at best and litigious at worst.

But taking a step back, what do we mean by knowing the customer? And how can we do it?

Three things are needed to really know the customer from the perspective of social media marketing (as we have described previously in this book)

a) First, the customer needs some incentive, whatever that may be to share their personal information. This assumes that all privacy guidelines and permissions are adhered to.

b) Secondly, we need an open ecosystem / platform. Factors like data portability are important to leverage the network effect and to enable operators to get others (third party developers) to do the work necessary to grow the ecosystem both in terms of content and new users. Initiatives like Google/Android and Facebook exploit this strategy best at the moment.

c) Finally, we need touch points, – places where the operator can interact directly with the customer and deliver the message (which could be in the form of an advertisement). Here again, open systems are important as a place where advertisements can

---

58   http://en.wikipedia.org/wiki/Call_detail_record

be placed. The call centre is a customer touch point, but it is an expensive touch point. Hence, operators need to make efforts to work with social networks, in order to collaborate and develop touch points such as the mobile web.

We also urgently require a system to manage all social media campaigns from an operator perspective. CDRs capture very limited information anyway – a lot more information is needed to complement the data captured. An alternate approach some operators attempt is to track user behaviour at a network level. The problems of network level tracking of user behaviour using mechanisms like the Phorm[59] system in the UK demonstrate why this will be such a pressing issue. The problem with network level tracking of user behaviour (even if you did get permission) is this: most people do not understand networks. And people do not trust what they do not understand.

So, there are advantages for telecoms network operators in working at higher levels of the stack rather than at the network level and also knowing the customer and engendering their trust rather than attempting to own the customer. This needs to happen in competition with the Web players who are already aggressive in this domain.

But, what about aggregated data?

By aggregated data we mean: The operator does not work with specific individuals or individual transactions – but rather with aggregates and data patterns derived from the data.

59 http://www.theregister.co.uk/2008/02/29/phorm_roundup/

> The understanding of data aggregates/ behavioural data patterns and the usage of this aggregated information is the key asset which a telecoms/mobile network operator does not currently utilise.

The understanding and utilization of these assets presents some important questions:

a) What are the guidelines/best practices?
b) What are the possible aggregates?(examples)
c) Who has done this successfully?
d) What kind of aggregates are valuable for the end client(buyers of advertising)?
e) How can aggregates be used apart from advertising?
f) How can data aggregates be used for market research?
g) How can data aggregates be used for predictive analysis i.e. anticipating user trends and behaviour?

The same principles of capturing customer behaviour at the application level could apply to the **converged telecoms layer**. Ownership of multiple customer access channels could provide the converged operator with a larger number of touch points through which they could know the customer in more detail. Thus, an operator who manages online, TV, IPTV, mobile and other related services could potentially gain a single view of the customer through the data harnessed from these channels.

From passive digital footprints to active digital footprints using social media marketing

As we have noted before, the effect of mobility is also very disruptive. We summarise the insights from the previous discussion:

- The mobile operator /provider has the opposite problem from the broadcaster. The former knows the customer individually but does not know much about that customer. Specifically they do not know the user's preferences which can be used to create a more personalised message (and by extension a message that is potentially useful to the receiver)
- So, the approach could be: Spot the patterns in data usage and validate the patterns using promotions. Execute this over as wide a network as possible(either a converged network or in partnership with a broadcast media channel)
- **Patterns**: Patterns in usage can be gleaned by merging data streams from outside the telecoms network along with telecoms data (CDRs). Consider program viewing schedules. Suppose an operator analyses the data based on program viewing schedules and discovers that at a certain time every week, a group of people on their network communicates via text message. If that time coincides with the transmission time of a specific program (say a TV serial) – then potentially these customers are fans of that serial and are communicating with each other as they watch the program.
- This information can be validated via **promotions** i.e. specific promotions designed to test the hypothesis with an opt in clause for further promotions.

- Finally, a telecoms provider can get insights if it **partners** with a TV station. They can also extend the scope of the network itself beyond mobile. This can be done by offering fixed network services, IPTV services etc – either on their own or in partnership.

- **The key is to get a single view of the customer from their data patterns** and/or to get an incrementally detailed view of their customer through the social interactions (who do they interact with) and behavioural interactions (what type of behaviour do they exhibit – which may need external data sources) – and then refine that analysis by specific promotions to validate the observations.

- The wider the network they can do this over (either on their own or in partnership) – the more effective the result. Over time, this process will lead to an understanding of the participant's **digital footprint** and to a transition from a passive digital footprint to an active digital footprint.

- There are two classifications for digital footprints: **Passive Digital Footprints** and **Active Digital Footprints**. A passive digital footprint is created when data is collected about an action without any client activation, whereas active digital footprints are created when personal data is released deliberately by a user for the purpose of sharing information about himself/herself. On the Web, many interactions leave a digital footprint such as creating a social networking profile, or commenting on a picture in Flickr. In a mobile context, CDRs are the transactional data that constitute the user's digital footprint.

- The question for providers is: How do we make the best use of digital footprints?

- Social media marketing campaigns are the driver to understanding the participant's digital footprint through a two stage process: Firstly to identify certain behavioural patterns in data and secondly to verify those observations by specific social media campaigns which seek to also get permission from the customers if possible
- Thus, we are starting with **Passive Digital Footprints** (based on behavioural data patterns) and transitioning to **Active Digital Footprints**(based on trust)

Xtract Social Links case study

The ideas discussed above can be implemented using the Xtract product set. The architecture of the Xtract XSL product is as shown below. Data from customer touch points is supplemented using external data feeds. This raw data is loaded in a central repository and the analytics and targeting engine creates insights on which specific campaigns are created based on behavioural and data patterns. The customer sees these campaigns through various touch points. The policy engine is used to configure and optimise the settings for the campaign. The output of the campaign is fed back to the system which creates a growing visibility of the customer over subsequent iterations.

The social network is created based on CDRs and the analysis gives insights on Alpha users, social neighbours and other social variables which is used in campaigns for product marketing, reducing churn and new customer acquisition. The feedback from the campaign enriches the operator's customer database.

     Ajit Jaokar, Brian Jacobs, Alan Moore and Jouko Ahvenainen

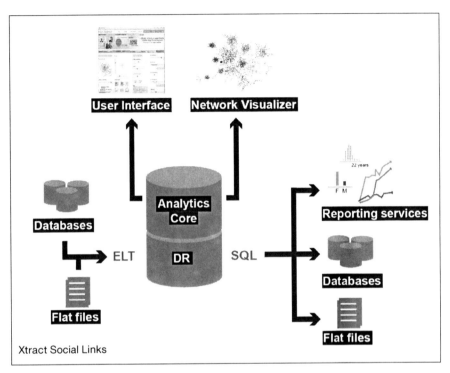

Xtract Social Links

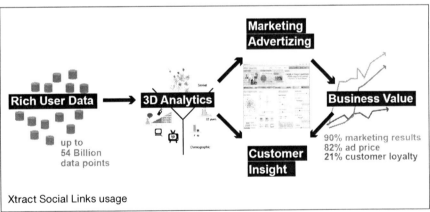

Xtract Social Links usage

In the next section, we will discuss how metrics play an important role in social media campaigns.

Social networks
– A data standpoint

In earlier sections, we have investigated and discussed social media marketing from three viewpoints: [1] Social Networks, [2] Traditional Media [3] Telecoms. Any analysis of social networks involves an understanding of the underlying data, and the relationships between the data. **Explicit data relationships** are easy to identify but are of limited use. **Implicit data relationships** – those driven by the underlying data depict a richer tapestry of the network but are relatively complex to identify. We illustrate this with the hypothetical example of the Nobel Prize winner with a poor online reputation.

The nobel prize winner with a poor online reputation

Many social network sites depend on explicit reputation mechanisms. These can be implemented in many ways such as the members rating each other 'Good' or providing testimonials. However, such explicit recommendations have limitations and can be 'gamed'. Later in this book, we discuss a data driven method of computing reputation. But here we illustrate the drawbacks of explicit reputation.

We call this the 'Nobel Prize winner with a poor reputation' problem.

If a person's 'reputation' depends on updating someone's site (or depends on my friends updating the site) – then it could mean: – '*If I win the Nobel Prize (which presumably means I am the best in my field) But I forget to update that site, then my reputation is low – irrespective of my achievements'.*

This is a simplistic example but it illustrates the concept. **Reputation** should be implicit and should be reflected by your actions (which in turn are captured in transactions/data), in other words reputation should be a byproduct of activities on a network. The concept of Reputation ties to members of the network who are valuable – for example Alpha Users (which we also discuss below).

An overview of online social networks

An online social network starts with a reflection of a person's real life person-to-person relationships taken into an online world. This is done through the simple mechanism of 'Profiles' and 'Friends'. In some cases, social networks may have specialized features and may be sometimes oriented towards specific tasks (such as LinkedIn for business networks) but their underlying mechanism always remains the same: social networks essentially consist of profiles and links. Of course, friends have other friends leading to the friend-of-a-friend (FOAF) concept[60] *(FOAF (an acronym of Friend-of-a-Friend) is a machine-readable ontology describing persons, their activities and their relations to other people and objects).*

More importantly, these next level relationships can also be reflected online and hence we have an extended social network that is more easily

---

60   http://en.wikipedia.org/wiki/FOAF_(software)

navigable in an online world than in a real life world. The practise of studying relationships and entities is called **Social Network Analysis**.

Adapted from Wikipedia, we can describe social network analysis as follows

A social network is a social structure made of nodes (which are generally individuals or organizations) that are tied by one or more specific types of interdependency, such as values, visions, ideas, financial exchange, friendship, kinship, dislike, conflict or trade. The resulting structures are often very complex. Social network analysis views social relationships in terms of nodes and links. Nodes are the individual actors within the networks, and links are the relationships between the actors. In its simplest form, a social network is a map of all of the relevant ties between the nodes being studied. The network can also be used to determine the social capital of individual actors. These concepts are often displayed in a graph, where nodes are the points and links are the lines.

Another definition comes from Valdis Krebs[61] *Social network analysis concerns itself with the measuring of relationships and flows between entities.*

Social networks – basic concepts

Social network analysis and social networking is based on some basic concepts. This section discusses a conceptual overview of social networks with a view to understanding the concepts. A more detailed discussion of social network analysis is included in the Appendix.

---

61   www.orgnet.com/sna.html

Social Networks: A social network is a social structure made of people (nodes) connected by different types of social interactions (such as communication, sharing similar interests, friendships etc). In other words, social networks depict how people are connected to each other. Social networks are everywhere where social interactions take place. This includes mobile communication, Facebook, online forums etc. In the telecoms world, social networks are often calculated from social interactions left behind by a digital footprint for example: in the case of mobile operators, CDRs (Call Detail Records) are the transactions that can be used to depict a social network.

The social interaction can be defined by the user ('who do I consider as my friends') or more accurately by their behaviour ('who am I actually in contact with'). Social networks include nodes (people) which are connected by links of different strengths. The same social network can look different if it is analysed at different times (business hours vs. evening hours for example) or from different data (all mobile communications vs. SMS network only).

Community: A community is a group of people who communicate relatively closely with each other or have similar interests. Communities may be of different sizes. One person may belong to several communities. One community can have many Alpha members (see below) and all members of a community may not be directly linked to each other, but can be as many as 3 links away from each other. Some communities form a tighter group where most individuals are linked to each other, other communities are looser, there are less and/or weaker inter-community connection.

Communities can be used in marketing for a personalised message ('Identify only communities with an average age below 25'), prediction ('if we know that 5 people in this community speak English, we can assume all people belonging to the community also speak English') or measuring of results ('how many people in a community tried the product following a campaign to the top 5% Alphas').

Link: A link refers to a social connection between two people. The stronger the connection between two people, the more important role it plays in forming the social network. The strength of the link is defined by volume, frequency and length of communication.

Friends: 'Friends' are the people a customer communicates with directly, they are one link away in the social network (1st tier). Friends refer to all the people a person communicates with directly, including their family, relatives, or business acquaintances. '2nd Tier Friends' refers to those people who are 2 links away from you. Targeting, prediction, and results measurement in the 1st and 2nd tier friends is typically more accurate than can be achieved by considering whole communities.

Sub-network: Sub-network is a sub-part of a network with interconnected people – for example it can be a social network formed only from SMS communications or a social network of people living only in the southern part of the country. Sub-networks are typically used for campaign measurement to divide the social network into separate parts (sub-networks) to assure comparability of different targeting approaches (analogous to 'test marketing'). The idea is to minimize contacts between different sub-networks to minimize random viral effects that can skew any comparison of different targeting approaches.

On-net: On-net individuals, are existing customers of for example, a mobile operator. These customers form a social network, since they communicate with each other. Typically most customers (up to 95%) are interconnected. However, there are also those customers who form small communities (with typically 1-5 people), isolated from any other on-net customers. On-net communication refers to communication within a mobile operator's network, between their existing customers.

Off-net: Off-net individuals communicate with the on-net customers but are not customers of the operator. Off-net communication refers to communication between on-net customers and your competitors' customers. Social networks can be formed either only on-net (if there is limited calculation capacity) or more accurately by combining on-net and off-net.

Alphas: Alpha users are influential individuals within a social network. Alphas usually have strong links to their many friends and occupy a central position in the social network. Being an Alpha does not necessarily mean being an early adopter, since the primary description of an Alpha is to have influence on other people. However, Alphas typically adopt products or services before others within their own social circle, and subsequently go on to recommend these products to others – assuming that is that they are interested in that product or service in the first place.

When choosing a target group for a marketing campaign, one has to decide how many users with the highest Alpha scores to target. There is no theoretical cut-off value for who is an Alpha and who is not; the relative order is more significant than the actual value. However, a good rule of thumb is to choose 2-5% of the customer base having the largest **Alpha scores (see below)**.

Sometimes it makes sense to use additional targeting criteria, depending on the product and campaign in question, in order to come up with the final target group. Alpha users do not necessarily communicate more than other customers. Although being an Alpha tends to correlate with larger volumes of communication, the nature of the communication and their position in the social network is what matters the most.

The **Alpha score** is a numerical value that ranks customers to different classes according to their level of influence (**Alpha score raw**). Customers in the highest class have the highest influence. In addition, we could complement the Alpha scores with specific Alphas.

Specific Alphas: Sometimes it is necessary to look beyond just generic influence (the Alpha score). Context related influence, taking into account the context of the customer's influence, typically leads to more accurate results. In other words, identification of the purpose specific Alphas takes into account whether the person is influential regarding whether or not the customer churns, buys a particular product or brand, and so on.

Purpose specific Alphas include **Churn Alphas, Product Alphas or Acquisition Alphas** (see below for more detailed definitions). Purpose specific Alphas should be used whenever possible, as targeting them usually increases campaigning accuracy more than targeting Alphas with a generic influence.

Churn Alpha: Churn propensity measures a customer's individual propensity to churn, or change from one telecom operator to another. One of the best indicators of churn is typically the number of churned friends. Churn Alpha is a customer that has a high propensity to churn as well as a high degree of influence on others to change operator. If a Churn Alpha churns, his friends are more likely to churn, too. Targeting Churn Alphas in a churn campaign thus minimizes overall churn in the customer base.

Churn Alpha Score is a churn propensity score that takes into account the customer's influence on others to churn. The score is relative to the number of persons that will not churn, if that person is prevented from leaving. The higher the score, the more indirect damage can be done if that person churns. Churn Alpha Score is then a combination of:

A customer's propensity to churn (Churn Propensity) and his/her influence on others to churn (Churn Influence Score).

Product Alpha: Product propensity measures a customer's individual propensity to start using (cross-sell), or increase the use of (up-sell) a specific product or service. Product Alpha is a customer that has a high tendency to buy the product or service and has a high influence in increasing usage among his friends as well. Product Alpha Score is a product propensity score that takes into account both a) the customer's own propensity to buy the product (Product Propensity) and b) his or her influence on others (Product Influence Score). The score is relative to the number of people that will take up the product, if the campaign is targeted to that individual.

Acquisition Alpha: Acquisition Alpha is a customer that has high propensity to acquire new members into the operator's network through a member-get-member campaign. They tend to be influential and have many off-net friends. The Acquisition Alpha score indicates the tendency of an individual to recruit new customers to the operator's network, if he/she is targeted in a member-get-member campaign.

Social networks – understanding the data behind social networks

Social network analysis starts with the data underlying the social network and then extends to finding the patterns/relationships in that data. Hence, an understanding of the data is the starting point for the study of social network analysis.

Significance of data

Given raw transactional data (for instance email data or instant messaging data or telecoms call records data); the first step is to create a **social graph** (we explain details of the Graph Theory in the Appendix) based on that data. A social graph is a graphical representation of all the people you know and how they are connected[62]. This is simply a case of assigning nodes to individuals and then to represent the relationship

---

62   http://www.readwriteweb.com/archives/social_graph_concepts_and_issues.php

between people by vertices (edges). A relationship could be inferred on the basis of messages exchanged; for instance if one email is exchanged between two nodes, we could represent that relationship as an edge. More emails between these nodes could indicate a stronger relationship and so on.

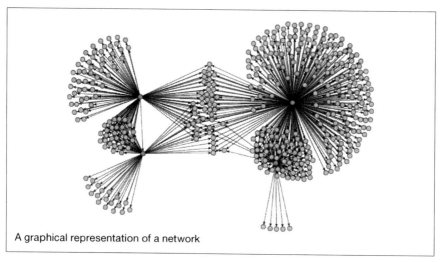

A graphical representation of a network

Given a community of people, a social network is a representation of the relationship between people. Thus, within a community, we can build more than one social network depending on the underlying rela-tionship between members of the community; for example a friendship network, a business network etc. Relationships between community members may be inferred by a number of ways by analyzing the data elements belonging to these members, for instance by analyzing their personal web pages, blogs, groups they belong to, the hierarchical struc-ture of their organization, the FOAF (friend of a friend) relationships[63], common resources shared, participation in newsgroups, forums , email

---

63   http://www.foaf-project.org/

communication, IM communication etc. The weight of the relationship depends on the number of different ways in which the two people are connected. For instance, two people may interact via email but in addition to this, they may also link each other's blog entries – which implies a stronger relationship.

Once the basic relationships have been identified, then it is a matter of identifying the most connected individuals (Alphas as we discussed before), those nodes with the highest connectivity and the highest weightage for the connections. (**Weightage** is a measure of the strength of the relationship along various parameters, for instance ratings). Once the data is modelled as a social network, a number of insights can be gleaned.

Analysis of online social networks

Data from social networks is structurally different from other networks, in particular the Web. Specifically, social networks have a much higher fraction of symmetric links and also exhibit much higher levels of local clustering. The growth of both the Web and social networks are governed by the **Power Law**. The Power Law is a term used to describe a phenomenon where large events are rare but small events are more common[64]. Many real life scenarios follow the Power Law – for instance there are many small earthquakes but few large earthquakes.

Like other networks that share Power Law growth processes, online social networks are governed by the theory of **preferential attachment** which implies that new nodes tend to attach themselves to already popular ones. Another concept that governs the growth of social net-

---

64   http://www.hpl.hp.com/research/idl/papers/ranking/ranking.html

works is the **Random Walk Principle**. In the Random Walk structure, nodes tend to make new friends with those with whom they already share friends by taking 'random walks'. We can see this 'random walk' behaviour in sites like Facebook and Twitter where new members start with a few friends who are already well connected and then see their friends to identify the next set of friends to connect to. These 'random walks' tend to select friends who are already likely to have other common friends. Thus, the network grows in a specific manner driven by the relationship between friends.

Social networks also display **scale free network characteristics**. Scale free networks are a type of Power Law network where the high degree nodes (nodes that have many links) tend to be connected to other high degree nodes. The degree distribution of online social networks follows the Power Law; there are a few very highly connected nodes and many sparsely connected nodes. Online social networks also display **small world characteristics**[65](small world networks are networks in which most nodes are not neighbors, but can be reached from every other node by a small number of hops or steps). Small world networks exhibit a high degree of **clustering**; in conventional language they tend to form cliques.

We also observe a **high degree of reciprocity in directed user links**, leading to a strong correlation between user **indegree** and **outdegree**. This differs from Web content graphs like the graph formed by Web hyperlinks, where the popular pages (**authorities – which have inbound links**) and the pages with many links (**hubs**) are distinct. Online social networks contain a large, **strongly connected core** of

---

[65] http://en.wikipedia.org/wiki/Small-world_network

high-degree nodes, surrounded by many small clusters of low-degree nodes. This suggests that high-degree nodes in the core are critical for the connectivity and the flow of information in these networks. Symmetry (or reciprocal links as discussed above) can also make it harder to identify reputable sources of information just by analyzing the network structure, because reputed sources tend to dilute their importance when pointing back to arbitrary users who link to them (often as a courtesy). Note that this behaviour is different from the Web since the Web does not exhibit this trait.

Groups are created by users with shared interests. Group sizes follow a Power-Law distribution, in which the vast majority has only a few users each. Groups represent tightly clustered communities of users in the social network. In addition, the members of smaller user groups tend to be more clustered than those of larger groups. Many of the small groups in these networks are **cliques**. Low-degree nodes tend to be part of very few communities, while high-degree nodes tend to be members of multiple groups. This implies a correlation between the link creation activity and the group participation.

We depict some social networks graphically overleaf

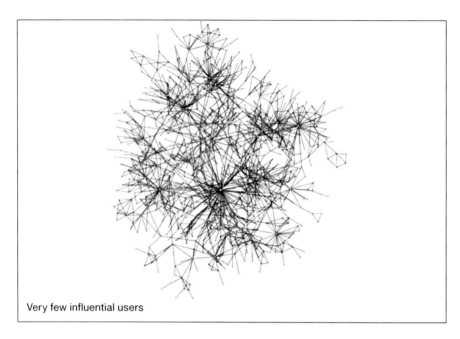

Very few influential users

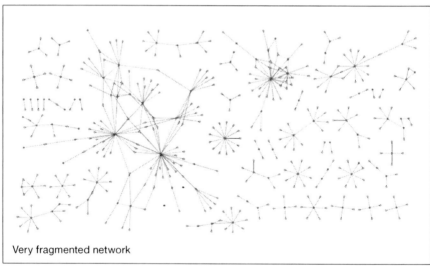

Very fragmented network

Ajit Jaokar, Brian Jacobs, Alan Moore and Jouko Ahvenainen

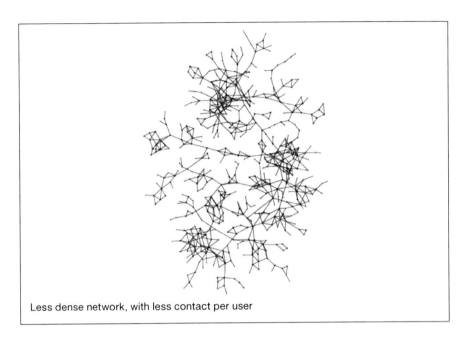

Less dense network, with less contact per user

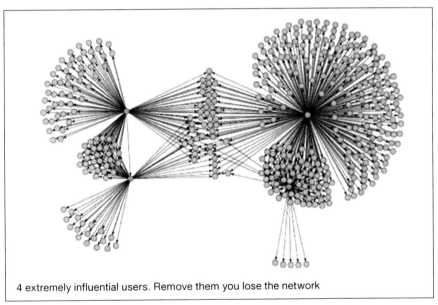

4 extremely influential users. Remove them you lose the network

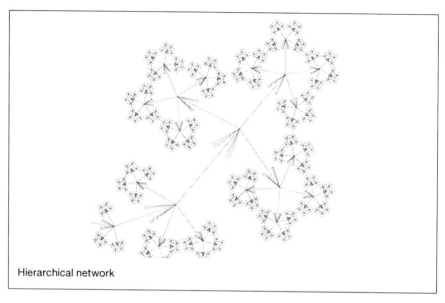

Hierarchical network

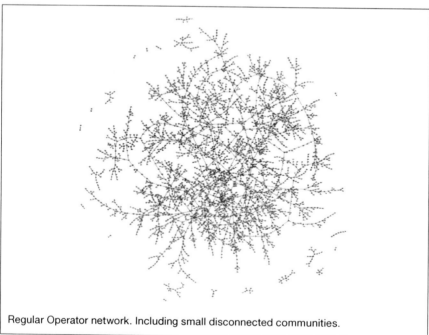

Regular Operator network. Including small disconnected communities.

Ajit Jaokar, Brian Jacobs, Alan Moore and Jouko Ahvenainen

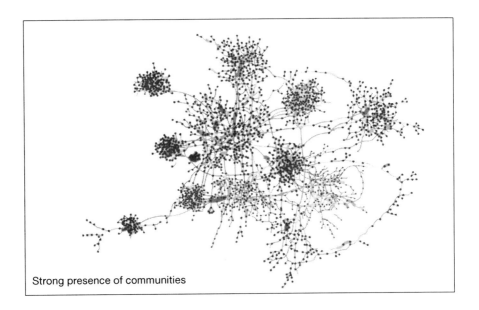

Strong presence of communities

Social network search

Having explored some aspects of social networks from a data standpoint, we now move on to social network search.

The Web is based on hyperlinks which are used for search. In contrast, in most cases no hyperlinks exist between content posted on social networks (videos, pictures, blogs etc) Where links do exist, they are created by the content creator to publicise the content. However, links exist between the people who view/interact with the content. Thus the mechanism of content propagation is related to social network propagation and relates to **recommendations**. Recommendations are often the main method of finding content on the social web. Recommendations can be **explicit recommendations** (friends recommending content) or **implicit recommendations** (the provider suggesting content based on related previous searches). In addition, keyword based search, Top 10, tags, ratings etc are also popular discovery mechanisms for content.

As we have noted before, social network links differ from Web links (in that they exhibit a high degree of reciprocity) and also the core structure of social networks is different from the Web. Specifically, the social web contains a large strongly connected component held together by nodes of a high degree which are also connected amongst themselves. A majority of paths are 'local' they are formed through work, geography and the like, it takes only a few random links between people who belong to different 'subsets' (a subset being a place of work, geography etc), to create the **small world effect**. Social network search is based on the ideas of a **Greedy Algorithm**.

A greedy algorithm is any algorithm that follows the problem solving approach of making the locally optimum choice at each stage with the hope of finding the global optimum.[66]. For example the famous **travelling salesman problem**[67] is a greedy algorithm problem. At each stage the salesman needs to decide to visit the next unvisited city nearest to the current city. In a social network context, every individual can use knowledge of only their own direct contacts with the objective of forwarding the message to the contact 'most likely' to be able to send it to the destination (for example for a search or for a recommendation). The likely paths for forwarding the message, identifying the 'next hop' could include sending to the 'Best Connected' node (since that node is likely to be known to most people); closest to the target in the organisational hierarchy or nodes which are physically close to each other (Geography). Here, 'organisation' can mean any external group i.e. an office, a club, the members of a golfing group etc.

---

66 Adapted from Wikipedia http://en.wikipedia.org/wiki/Greedy_algorithm
67 http://en.wikipedia.org/wiki/Travelling_salesman_problem

　　　　Ajit Jaokar, Brian Jacobs, Alan Moore and Jouko Ahvenainen

Identification of sub communities within a network

Having identified the main actors and the relationships between the communities and understood the mechanisms driving social network content propagation, we now discuss the identification of sub communities within the network.

Informal networks called **communities of practice** can emerge within an organization as a result of communication between its members. These communities are based around a common goal or a purpose and coexist within the formal structure of an organization. Since these informal relationships can be useful for a number of real life problems, their identification based on real life data is desirable. They are not identified in advance or through formal means like surveys and questionnaires **but rather as a property of the information that is generated from their interaction.**

The first step is to create a graph based on the data. This is simply a case of assigning nodes to individuals and to represent the relationship between people by vertices (edges). This can be done by iteratively identifying all '**betweenness relationships'** within a social network

('Betweenness' is the extent to which a nodes lies between other nodes in the network. It takes into account the connectivity of the node's neighbors. Nodes with high 'betweenness' are nodes which bridge clusters of other nodes. It reflects the number of people a person is connecting indirectly through their direct links.)

In the above figure, we see a number of sub-groups and also links between these groups. If these links were to be removed, the groups would be isolated. If we progressively identify all such sub-networks or sub-groups, we will decompose the main social network into a series of sub- networks.

Reputation and trust

The final topic in understanding social networks from a data standpoint is to understand **Reputation** and **Trust.** Reputation and trust are important since they are the foundations of so many other elements within social networks. For instance product recommendations follow a trusted path, Alpha users have a high reputation and are trusted and so on. Trust and reputation are relevant to social media marketing for three reasons:

a) Content flows along trusted paths (recommendations)
b) A trusted node (profile) is more valuable than a non-trusted node from both a social and a commercial perspective
c) Trust and reputation can now be quantified through online social networks. Hence, a computation of trust and reputation is now possible – which is different from the pre- social network era .

However, trust and reputation are not easy to define, let alone quantify. Trust and reputation can be defined as:[68]

---

68   Trust and Reputation Model in Peer-to-Peer Networks Yao Wang, Julita Vassileva

> *Trust* – a peer's belief in another peer's capabilities, honesty and reliability *based on its own direct experiences*; *Reputation* – a peer's belief in another peer's capabilities, honesty and reliability *based on recommendations* received from other peers. Reputation can either be centralized (like eBay reputation or a credit score system), or it can be decentralized; computed locally and then aggregated.

Characteristics of Trust: Trust and reputation are used to evaluate the trustworthiness of a node. They have the following characteristics:

a) They are specific to a context: for example we may trust a doctor for medical reasons but not to fix a car

b) Trust and reputation are multi faceted: They are based on a number of characteristics of the person being evaluated i.e. We may trust a specific characteristic of a person and at the same time distrust other characteristics of the same person

c) Dynamic: Trust and reputation are dynamic; they may change over time

d) Trust is asymmetric i.e. if person A trusts person B, that trust may not be reciprocated

e) Trust is not necessarily transitive. If person A trusts person B, and if person B trusts person C, then it does not follow that person A trusts person C.

Evaluation of trust: The evaluation of trustworthiness itself can be multifaceted; we can identify five facets of trust[69]

a) The feedback a peer obtains from other peers: or direct transactional feedback

b) The feedback scope, such as the total number of transactions that a peer has with other peers. The proportion of positive feedback is more important, he average rating over a range of transactions with a reflection of the total number of transactions

c) The credibility factor for the feedback source: how credible is the source giving the feedback

d) The transaction context factor: for instance a few mission critical transactions are more important than a number of smaller, less important transactions and

e) The community context factor for addressing the community:For instance, only a few nodes in a community may actually give feedback, thus skewing the reputation mechanism in the whole community.

Calculation of Trust: Trust can be calculated using a range of models[70] (Note that while these are peer-to-peer models, the same principles can be applied in other scenarios):

a) Central Control Model through 'leader peers': This technique is used in certificate management and the leader peers are assigned

---

69   PeerTrust: Supporting Reputation-Based Trust for Peer-to-Peer Electronic Communities
70   A p2p global trust model based on recommendation zhen zhang1, xiao-ming wang1, yun-xiao wang2

digital certificates by the Certifying Authority (CA). Public Scheme architecture (PKI) is an example of such a scheme[71].

b) Local Based Recommendation Model: In this model, one node asks a group of other local nodes to obtain trust information about the target node (the node whose reputation is being evaluated). The dependence on local trust is a limitation of this model but the advantage is that the method operates on a partial trust graph.

c) Digital Signature Model: This model relates to the integrity of a file (content) and does not care about assigning trust to the sender of the file. When a file (content) is used and is found to be good, the user would sign the file with a positive rating based on a private key. The more positive feedback the file has, the greater its positive reputation.

d) Global Based Recommendation Model: In this model, a peer's trust is defined through the evaluation of all the peers that transact with it.

The propagation of content in social networks

Having now studied social networks in detail from a data perspective, we now look at some of the insights from existing social networks.

Note that this section has been derived from research papers and you should read the following notes in the context of the findings from these papers.

---

71   http://en.wikipedia.org/wiki/Public_key_infrastructure

Notes:

a) **The problem of data collection:** The problem of data collection is complex and non trivial in any social media research. There are a number of possibilities to capture raw data – each with their own advantages and disadvantages. For instance, one could monitor all data from a widget on a profile page or from a passive probe. Another alternative is to integrate with the social network at a database level via a programmatic interface to the underlying database. The third alternative is to take the 'snippet of code' approach taken by Google analytics[72] within which the object we want to monitor should include a small section of code which captures the transactional information. The client side approaches (non database approaches) are relatively simple to implement since a database approach needs complex and expensive integration which varies upon different sites and needs to cater to different formats. This is the same problem as the ETL task in traditional data warehousing.

b) **Use of research papers:** Since social media analytics is an emerging topic, we have drawn heavily upon research papers. It is important to note that 'proof' is a harsh word when it comes to social media research. In other words, a research paper merely validates a certain hypothesis (the research question) based on observations upon a set of data. To mitigate this risk, we have focussed on research papers published at major conferences (hence they are subjected to extensive peer review) and /or chosen research papers that work with very large volumes of data.

---

72 http://www.google.com/analytics/

For instance, in the paper *Analysis of Topological Characteristics of Huge Online Social Networking Services*, YongYeol Ahn et al analyse the entire Cyworld social network's friend relationships (191 million friend relationships among 12 million users). Any insights gained from such papers are unique and useful. However, all research paper analysis should be considered with the caveats as above: a research paper is a set of observations on a specific data set and other datasets could give other results. Hence, any conclusions are indicative but not universal.

c) **Sampling techniques:** Social network analytics is not an exact science. Indeed, it is a subjective science and is based on sampling of a target population. Sampling techniques and the sample data size play an important part in the results as we have discussed in the choice of papers. The crawling (data gathering) techniques used in collecting information may themselves introduce an element of bias. At each step in the crawling process, we can obtain a set of links into and out of a specific node. The challenge lies in covering the entire connected component. Algorithms like **breadth-first search (BFS)** and **depth-first search (DFS)** are used to sample data. A discussion of these algorithms is beyond the scope of this book – but the concept should be borne in mind that sampling techniques themselves introduce a subjective element

d) **Loss of temporal analysis:** One drawback of social media analysis is that the analysis is done on data snapshots. Hence, the temporal (time based) view of the analysis is lost. This problem can be addressed by taking snapshots of the same information over time and then comparing the metrics from the snapshots. Some data does not change rapidly and may not need temporal analysis (for example historical analysis of trends). However, in general, we expect that metrics will be calculated on a time-based analysis and indeed are time bound (since the social graph itself changes rapidly). The data collection method used plays an important role here – for instance an ongoing transactional analysis gives an almost real time picture of the metric. However, if data needs to be first extracted and transformed, then the computation of the metric needs considerable time in itself, which needs to be factored into the final result.

Keeping the above caveats in mind, some insights from existing social networks are listed below. These insights can be used to compute social media metrics and can be retrospectively applied to any social network. Relevant papers have been referenced below in the text or in the footnote.

Flickr[73] – (www.flickr.com)
   a) Users who already have many links, tend to create more links
   b) Users who receive an incoming link tend to respond with a link back to the source
   c) Users who are already close to each other tend to link to each other
   d) Over four out of five photos in Flickr were located by traversing the social network links

---

73 Growth of the Flickr Social Network Alan Mislove et al

YouTube: (www.youtube.com) RSS feeds, web reviews, blogs, e-mails, or other recommendation web sites are some of the mechanisms used to find content on **YouTube**. There exist extremely heavy publishers in UGC, who will post over 1,000 videos over a few years. [74]

Cyworld: (www.cyworld.com) **Dunbar's number** represents the approximate size of the community that a person can manage; it is said to be around 150. While online social network members collect hundreds or even thousands of friends, in the paper Analysis of Topological Characteristics of Huge Online Social Networking Services, YongYeol Ahn et al observe from a study of **Cyworld** network that the testimonial network (i.e. the number of testimonials received and given) may well represent a true measure of the social network for an individual – and not the number of online friends that they have.

Facebook applications: (www.facebook.com) In the paper 'Poking Facebook: Characterization of OSN Applications' Minas Gjoka, et al characterize the popularity and user reach of Facebook applications. Their analysis is based on an analysis of usage data gathered over a period of six months from Facebook and Adonomics – a Facebook analytics service. They also crawl publicly accessible Facebook user profiles and obtain per-user application installation statistics, for approximately 300K users and 13.6K applications. Their findings indicate that (i) the popularity of Facebook applications has a highly skewed distribution; (ii) although the total number of application installations increases with time, the

---

74 Understanding UGC content I Tube, You Tube, Everybody Tubes: Analyzing the World's Largest User Generated Content Video System

average user activity decreases; and (iii) users with more applications installed are more likely to install new applications.

They categorise the 7 most popular categories of applications in Facebook as:

1) Friend Comparison: Applications that include comparing best friends and comparing traits of friends.
2) Casual Communication: Applications that allow users to exchange messages and write on each other's wall.
3) Rating, Taste Matching and Recommendations: Used to review, compare and recommend music, restaurants etc.
4) Gestures: Includes applications that allow users to perform virtual gestures (poke, bite etc).
5) Self Expression: Used to express moods, political opinions etc.
6) Gifting: Enabling users to exchange virtual gifts.
7) Meeting People: For example online dating etc.(of particular interest)

Thus we see that social factors and casual communications dominate. Facebook also finds that throughout the period of their study, the most popular items remained popular, which means that although applications continue to be developed, they exhibit Long Tail[75] characteristics.

Geography and social networks: When finding the next node to foreword a message to, **geography** and occupation are the most important dimensions and geography dominates in the early stages[76]

---

75   http://en.wikipedia.org/wiki/The_Long_Tail
76   Geographical routing in social networks Geographic routing in social networks David Liben-Nowell

Twitter: Users can be classed into broadcasters (who have many followers), acquaintances (those who exhibit reciprocity, or a similar number of followers as following) and miscreants (spammers, evangelists and the like who tend to contact as many people as they can)[77]

Spread of information through social links in Flickr: An examination of the **spread of information through social links in Flickr** provides some interesting observations[78]. There are a number of mechanisms by which users locate sites like Flickr.

Examples are:
- **Strategically** placed content on the front page of Flickr, top 100, most viewed etc.
- **External** links from blogs etc.
- **Search results** for specific content from search engines.
- **Links** between content on the same site. Through a social network by sharing content but also by subscribing to feeds, favourite photos etc.

Unlike the spread of most infectious diseases, the structure of Flickr suggests an interesting epidemiological phenomenon:[79]

A user will retain the same favourite indefinitely – there is no recovery – unless he removes the photo from his favourite list. While users can have

---

77 A Few Chirps About Twitter Balachander Krishnamurthy et al
78 Characterizing Social Cascades in Flickr Meeyoung Cha, Alan Mislove, Ben Adams and Krishna P. Gummadi
79 Characterizing Social Cascades in Flickr Meeyoung Cha, Alan Mislove, Ben Adams and Krishna P. Gummadi

multiple favourites, as the number of photos marked as favourites grows, the bookmarked photos are paged such that older ones have less chance of exposure to other users. For such pictures, the user effectively becomes no longer infectious and can be placed in the removed category.

Also, while highly connected nodes are more likely to widely disseminate a picture, they are also likely to replace that picture with a different favourite very rapidly. So their transmission rate is high, but the duration of infection is short. Conversely, weakly connected nodes may have low transmission potential but a long duration of infection. The nodes that transmit most efficiently over long time periods may thus be of intermediate connectivity.

Digg: (www.digg.com) An analysis of Digg reveals that stories that spread outside the submitter's neighbourhood tend to go on to be very popular. The effect is consistent in early stages; it is observed that stories that went on to spread outside the submitter's neighbourhood in early stages went on to be popular[80].

---

80   Analysis of Social Voting Patterns on Digg Kristina Lerman et al

Social media marketing metrics

As media became more fragmented, as the number of consumer touch-points increased, and as our economies became more mature, the pressure on marketing to become more accountable has gone up and with that, has increased the demand for measurement.

John Hagel writing in 'Shift Happens' The Future of Advertising [81] points out that:

In the advertising world, multiple shifts are piling on top of each other and it is often hard to keep track of them, much less understand their implications. For instance:

- Shifts from advertising placed in digital content to ads placed in social networks and applications
- Shifts from digital advertisements delivered through conventional PCs to a growing array of mobile devices with an increasing ability to target messages based on the physical location of the person
- Shifts in the behaviour of digital users and in their responsiveness to advertisements online

---

81   http://edgeperspectives.typepad.com/edge_perspectives/2008/03/shift-happens-t.html

- Shifts in the way companies connect with and build relationships with stakeholders (for example, blurring boundaries between customers, partners, and suppliers)
- Shifts in the revenue models for businesses, as online businesses in particular become more and more dependent on advertising as a key revenue source (for example, is there any Web 2.0 start-up that doesn't blithely answer 'advertising' when asked about their revenue model?)

With this entire shift comes a need for greater and more complex measurement and a greater need for accountability. In addition, the nature of advertising may be changing at its core and **advertising could be treated as a service**. Let's take local advertising as a service. The classified market broadly breaks down into:

- Cars
- Property
- Renting
- Jobs

An example might be a service which we could call 'First in the Queue.' (services similar to this do exist). Within this service, the consumer signs up for a mobile service and registers that he is specifically interested in this car, and/or this property with this spec, within this budget. The local newspaper that runs the service aggregates this information, and sends it to the user and maybe to a small network of his friends – who might be flat hunting.

New services like these could become commonplace and could contribute to the shift towards a greater degree of dialogue and sharing than is currently happening within the advertising industry.

Notwithstanding the changes in the media/advertising landscape, metrics have always been important, even for traditional media. We have seen the issues with the concept of metrics in relation to social media. In this section, we explore the actual idea of social media metrics.

By definition, a social media metric is numerical and measurable. Metrics can serve many purposes in relation to social media. Presented below are the characteristics of social media metrics:

a) Social media metrics (from our convergence perspective) span platforms.

b) Social media metrics use many of the principles of data analytics we have discussed before – for instance reputation, propogation of content etc.

c) Social media metrics may be used in social media campaigns.

d) Social media metrics may be indicative and not absolute. For instance, we may not be able to compare one social network with another in terms of metrics but we may be able to progressively know more about a specific social network by monitoring metrics for that network.

Social media metrics may be used for the following

a) For valuing social media and for audience exchange

b) For product development through social media campaigns

c) For market research

d) For prediction

e) For campaign planning

f) For post campaign evaluation

g) To make marketing accountable and measurable.

h) Increase the (value) cost of ads delivered to digital platforms.

i) Reduce churn

j) Increase customer loyalty

k) Launch new products and services in the marketplace at greater speed and lower cost

l) Enable highly effective virality within social networks

m) Effectively monetize digital communities

n) Significantly reduce marketing costs

In this book, we identify the following metrics for social media marketing:

- Who they are: **Alphas** (alternate terms – **personal CPM**)
- Who they influence: **Engagement factor** (alternate terms – **recommendations, viral effects**)
- Predictive metrics:'What if' scenarios
- Subset metrics: Geography, Long tail, Youth, others

We also discuss two other metrics: **Cost per Relevant Audience** and **Universal Profiles**

If we distil the above metrics, we get three underlying themes:

- How valuable is a person within a social media context?
- What is the downstream impact of this person within their social graph?
- How does content flow within a social graph?

          Ajit Jaokar, Brian Jacobs, Alan Moore and Jouko Ahvenainen

All these problems can be modelled as social network scenarios. For instance, the value of a person within a social media advertising context is a 'distributed reputation' problem; the downstream impact of this person is a social graph navigation problem and the flow of content is a viral propagation problem. Within the context of the above themes, we can calculate all the metrics; for instance, 'Geography' becomes a special case of recommendation (An example can be finding out who recommends a product within a specific geography).

Hence, the principles we discussed in the previous sections directly apply to the computation of metrics. In all cases though, we need to start first with the data as we look to track conversations across platforms.

Alpha users

We have discussed Alpha users in detail earlier . We revisit the definitions from the previous sections.

Alphas: Alpha users are the influential peoples in a social network. Alphas usually have strong links to their many friends and a central position in the social network. Being an Alpha does not necessarily mean being an early adopter, since the primary description of an Alpha is to have influence on other people. However, Alphas are typically amongst the first within their social circle to adopt products or services, and recommend the products to others – assuming they are interested in that product/service in the first place.

When choosing a target group for a marketing campaign, one has to decide how many users with the highest Alpha scores are targeted. There is no theoretical cut-off value for who is, or is not, an Alpha; the relative order is more significant than the actual value. However, a good rule of thumb is to choose 2-5% of the customer base having the largest **Alpha scores**.

Sometimes it makes sense to use additional targeting criteria, depending on the product and campaign in question, in order to come up with the final target group. Alpha users do not necessarily communicate more than other customers. Although being an Alpha tends to correlate with larger volumes of communication, the nature of the communication and their position in the social network is what matters the most.

The **Alpha score** is a numerical value that ranks customers to different classes according to their level of influence (**Alpha score raw**). Customers in the highest class have the highest influence. In addition, we could complement the Alpha scores with specific Alphas.

The **Alpha score** is a combination of a user's social links and position in the network and her/his propensity to do something, e.g. buy a product or react to marketing. The key components of the alpha score are strengths of the links to social neighbors and a campaign specific propensity score. Each user has a propensity score that is calculated from his earlier behavior and behavior similar to other users and social network neighbours. The strength of the links indicate a person's influence on other people in the network. The stronger the link, the higher the degree of influence. The strengths are calculated from the amount and quality of communication (like the length of calls, number of messages, number of recommendations) and historical campaign results. Then the Alpha score is calculated by estimating the total influence in the network, and if a certain user belongs within the target group.

Specific Alphas: Sometimes it is necessary to look beyond just generic influence (Alpha score). Context-related influence or taking into account the context of the customer's influence, typically leads to more accurate results. In other words, identification of purpose-Specific Alphas takes into account whether the person is influential in terms of churning, buying a particular product, and so on.

Purpose Specific Alphas include **Churn Alphas, Product Alphas or Acquisition Alphas** (see below for more detailed definitions). Purpose specific Alphas should be used whenever possible, as targeting purpose specific Alphas usually increases campaigning accuracy more than targeting Alphas with a generic influence.

Churn Alpha: Churn propensity measures a customer's individual propensity to churn. One powerful indicator of churn is the number of churned friends. Churn Alpha is a customer with a high propensity to churn as well as a high degree of influence on others to change operator. If a Churn Alpha churns, his friends are more likely to churn, too. Targeting Churn Alphas in a churn campaign thus minimises the overall churn in the customer base.

Churn Alpha Score is a churn propensity score that takes into account the customer's influence on others to churn. The score is relative to the number of people who will not churn, if that key, influencing person is prevented from leaving. The higher the score, the more indirect damage can be done if that person churns. The Churn Alpha Score is thus a combination of:

A customer's own propensity to churn (Churn Propensity) and his/her influence on others to churn (Churn Influence Score).

Product Alpha: Product propensity measures a customer's individual propensity to start using (cross-sell), or increase the use of (up-sell) a specific product or service. Product Alpha is a customer that has a high tendency to buy the product or service and has a high degree of influence in increasing usage among his friends as well. The Product Alpha Score is a product propensity score that takes into account both a) the customer's own propensity to buy the product (Product Propensity) and b) his/her influence on others (Product Influence Score). The score is relative to the number of other people that will take up the product, if the campaign is targeted to that individual.

Acquisition Alpha: Acquisition Alpha is a customer that has a high propensity to acquire new members into the operator's network through a member-get-member campaign. They tend to be influential and have many off-net friends. Acquisition Alpha Score indicates the tendency of an individual to recruit new customers to the operator's network, if he/she is targeted in a member-get-member campaign.

Alpha User and Alpha Score are two simple examples to measure and utilize social marketing intelligence. There are also several other models to utilize Alpha Score information, e.g. Alpha Community. This is a community where many people have high Alpha Scores. The notion of the Alpha Community becomes important when a marketer wants to market products that have a high network effect (s these products acquire a high value when your friends use it). Mobile services like mobile email and games fit into this category. In these cases marketing should be first targeted to these Alpha Communities and the get critical mass there. Alpha Community is an example built around the concept of Alpha scoring, and is not only about finding individuals.

Ajit Jaokar, Brian Jacobs, Alan Moore and Jouko Ahvenainen

Profiles

In a strict sense, profiles are not 'metrics'. However, in the context of social media marketing, profiles can have monetary value – either in themselves as a source of placement of advertisement, or in the form of an advertisement exchange or in the form of viral influence (the ability to influence others within their social graph). When we refer to 'Profiles' we are referring to a richer 'Three dimensional' profile which incorporates demographics behaviour and social positioning. We explain this idea in the following diagram

We no longer have 'static profiles'. Instead we have living/ dynamic profiles which evolve based on data at any given time.

Profiles incorporate:

- Demographic data (which is static)
- Behaviour transactions data and
- Social interactions data.

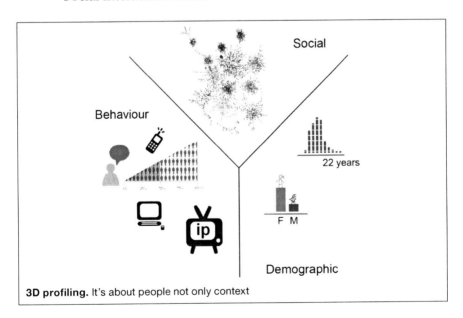

3D profiling. It's about people not only context

We extend the idea of 3D **profiles (or dynamic profiles)** to the idea of **universal profiles.** The idea of universal profiles arises as an enhancement to other existing profiling mechanisms. For example, in the UK, Mosaic(now part of Experian) classifies UK households into one of 61 types and 11 groups. The Mosaic groups are as listed below:

1) Symbols of Success
2) Happy Families
3) Suburban Comfort
4) Ties of Community
5) Urban Intelligence
6) Welfare Borderline
7) Municipal Dependency
8) Blue Collar Enterprise
9) Twilight Subsistence
10) Grey Perspectives
11) Rural Isolation

The same idea could be adopted for social network profiles. In that sense, they become universal and understood across the industry, **but the critical difference is that although they use the same or similar data-points to classify people, these are not one time snapshots but rather a dynamic system that can measure changes and trends over time.**

    Ajit Jaokar, Brian Jacobs, Alan Moore and Jouko Ahvenainen

Cost per relevant audience

The idea of universal profiles and dynamic/3D profiles extends to the next metric: **Cost per relevant audience,** a notion first advanced by Alan Moore.

All media is bought, sold, measured, and quantified by the CPM model. **Cost Per Thousand** (CPM, where M is the Roman numeral for thousand, is also often referred to as CPT), incorporates the cost of the space or time, and Gross Rating Points (GRPs) as a quantitative measurement of the audience reached. In the case of on-line media forms we have Cost Per Click (CPC), which ignores the characteristics of the audience doing the clicking. CPM as an approach is really the only truly universal way by which the value of audiences could be quantified – and measured even remotely accurately.

We contend that CPM does not really work in the world of social media. CPM is a very broad measure of audience reached (however defined) for cost paid. Thus it is really about impressions pushed down to the audience, not influence or engagement built from the audience up. As we have seen, social media is all about connections, influence and engagement,. Of course, there are also terms and metrics like CTR (Click through rates), CPA (cost per access), CPC (Cost per click) etc – but they all measure actions which can perhaps come multiple times from the same person.

There is room for taking the old CPM definition and extending it to measure how many people are truly reached, as defined by their observed behaviour, thus delivering a real Cost **Per Audience**. As with traditional media, CPM's definition also includes those who are less relevant to the advertiser. The idea can be extended to mirror the old cost-per-target-group idea with the overlay of basing the calculation on people's real behaviour as opposed to averages from survey results; so that advertiser can start by stating that they will only pay for those members of the audience who are of true relevance to them.

Online media forms have lagged behind traditional media by selling pages, not audiences. We believe that this has to change if the medium (we use the word in the broadest sense) is to fulfill its revenue potential.

So what we are proposing here is a mixing of the old idea, of buying audience, with the new idea of true accountability in terms of understanding the important characteristics of the audience reached, and then by measuring the most relevant (to the advertiser) audience behaviour.

We can illustrate this from a brand perspective, with a hypothetical example: The client gives an agency a brief. The brief might be to sell more units of Coca-Cola. The marketing people along with the agency do an analysis of the market research data available and identify that the best way of doing that is ; by not selling more Coke to those who already buy Coca-Cola and not Pepsi; nor by trying to convert loyal Pepsi users, **but to sell more Coke to those that waver between the two brands**.

Hence, the target market might be something like: heavy and medium users of Colas, who choose Coke on 50% or less occasions when they choose to drink a Cola. The agency will start to turn this into a description, or data that they can use to select different communication forms. The planners will use multiple data sources to do this – like TGI[82], or proprietary studies available only to the agency, or Coke's own market research, plus media consumption data. The aim at this stage is

82   http://www.tgisurveys.com/whatis/

to select media forms – TV, magazines, social media, etc, as opposed to specific vehicles.

The customer's 3D profiles fits here. The planner's skill is in translating the business need, and the overall communications need into something that looks like a plan. For example – one of the characteristics of the members of this target market is that they are heavy mobile phone users, and they spend time blogging and on social media sites. *The 3D profiles will merge the data sources from which this insight emerges into a tool that will help the planner select the type of media form most likely to deliver results.* The tool will also identify and quantify the various segments that make up the overall target market.

Thus, we are now looking at a relevant audience – or an audience that is relevant to the task in hand (it is no doubt entirely irrelevant to any other task). There is a cost attached to each element that makes up the plan – so it is easy to calculate the CPRA.

Another way to think of this is to explore the idea of a **'Just in Time'** network. Buyers want choice and the creation of a federated set of profiles which spans multiple networks is appealing to advertisers. We can view such a network as a Just in Time network created to fulfill a specific requirement often at a short notice – for instance who are the Chinese speaking people in the USA in the week before the Beijing Olympics? (at whom we might target a special promotion to 'call home').

In practise, the CPRA idea may be implemented as an **exchange for audiences** (see below for more on Audience Exchanges) or it may be implemented as a concept over a set of slides. For instance, a publisher has 7 websites, yet it struggles to sell inventory evenly across all 7 as advertisers want to guarantee that they can reach women 18 - 40 on 3 of those sites. Hence inventory is left unsold. However, with the concept of CPRA, it is possible to identify a specific audience across the sites.

As unsophisticated and unreliable as traditional media measurement approaches may have been in the past, they did provide standards and currencies that enabled marketers, buying agencies, and media companies to transact business. Today, this equilibrium has become unstable. Marketers demand more effectiveness and efficiency from their media buys. Digital media are reaching a critical mass with consumers. And the promise of more granular (or even real-time) data capture of consumer response to advertising is tantalizingly close to realisation through concepts like CPRA.

To conclude, the cost per relevant audience (CPRA) is a mechanism to identify the most relevant audience that is most likely to be the best receivers, adopters, and disseminators of a particular commercial message. This audience may not exist within a specific network but may actually span multiple networks (here a 'network' could mean social networks or web sites).

Auction or dynamic pricing is an important part of the CPRA concept. Google has been successful in using auctions for search advertising. Similarly in social media, publishers sell audiences to advertisers. In the social media case, the auction is not about search words, but about audiences. If a certain audience is very popular among advertisers, it must be more expensive to reach this audience (a concept exploited over many years by the UK TV companies via the pre-empt system of buying and selling; in effect a blind auction within the framework of a rate-card). Otherwise targeting and the CPRA concept do not make sense for publishers.

Other metrics

In this section, we briefly touch on some other metrics. We have already discussed these before. For instance: the notion of an engagement factor indicates who the person influences. Engagement factors are synonymous with recommendations or viral effects.

Similarly, metrics can be predictive; they can predict a scenario based on historical data patterns and by analysing data. A variant of a predictive metric could be a 'What if' scenario – which is a hypothetical scenario based on a situation.

Finally, we could consider 'subset' metrics i.e. any metric applied to a specific data subset –for instance Geography or Youth.

It is easier to explain the metrics in terms of their usage – which we do in the next section.

Usage of metrics: Metrics in action

To illustrate the usage of the metrics discussed before, we consider the following examples. These examples are based on the product XSL (Xtract Social Links [83]) from Xtract Corporation. Xtract Social Links turns raw customer data into a marketing tool for mobile network Operators. XSL identifies the underlying network structures within the subscriber base and finds the most influential people, or Alpha Users. The result is a conceptual new layer of customer activity on top of the raw data. We discuss three cases:

- Churn reduction
- New customer acquisition
- Launch of new products

---

83   http://www.xtract.com/products/xsl/

Churn Management: Enables the reduction of churn in communities (or, it reduces customers leaving the community/network), by finding people at high risk to churn as well as those churners likely to influence individuals around them. Churn is known to be a highly viral phenomenon. The propensity to churn is predicted by taking into account traditional variables such as usage data and demographics together with variables derived from social network analysis. It is also able to identify'Churn Alphas', those individuals who have a high probability to churn, but as highly individual people, will also pull others with them. These people are obviously very important targets for any customer retention effort.

So, as a first step, Xtract Social Links creates a new social network and then calculates each subscriber's churn risks (churn score/ churn alphas) and then the subscriber's contextual influence on the network (total churn score). It then constructs a behaviour pattern analysis of the Churn Hubs (people with high churn alphas) and creates a churn report. Based on the churn report, specific campaigns can be run which will be targeted to reduce churn. For instance: make direct calls to top 40% of the target group and send direct email and SMS campaigns to the next 60% of the target group.

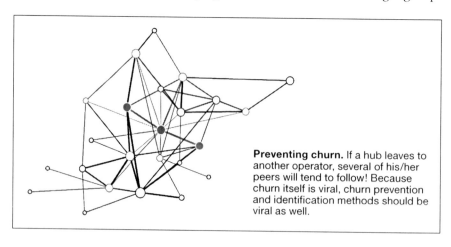

Preventing churn. If a hub leaves to another operator, several of his/her peers will tend to follow! Because churn itself is viral, churn prevention and identification methods should be viral as well.

Ajit Jaokar, Brian Jacobs, Alan Moore and Jouko Ahvenainen

Customer Acquisition : The aim of Customer Acquisition is to find the best targets for **member-get-member** campaigns, producing better results compared to traditional approaches. Word-of-mouth has proven to be the greatest influencing factor when choosing a telecommunications provider. Based on communication data (CDR's), we are able to identify people with the highest propensity for successfully recruiting more customers into the mobile operator's network – **the Acquisition Alphas**. In this case, Xtract Social Links calculates each customer's **propensity to bring in new customers** (Acquisition score) and conducts a behaviour pattern analysis of the Acquisition Hubs from which an acquisition report is generated.

Product Marketing: The success of any viral marketing campaign – whether it is product up-sell, cross-sell or launching a new product – is highly dependent on the targeting of the most influential customers. Xtract Social Links creates a target list of subscribers that are able to create the highest total pull in the communities.

Customer Insight : Increases the amount and depth of information on an individual customer as well as in a group level. It utilizes the underlying social network to predict unknown attributes for individual customers. For example the client is able to predict customer demographics such as age and gender for the whole customer subset or indeed to gain insight into specific customer behaviour.

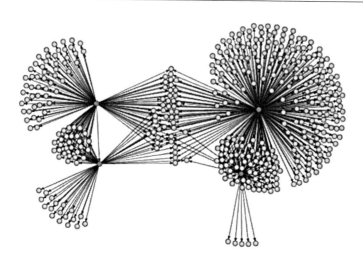

a) Recommendation network of a Manga book

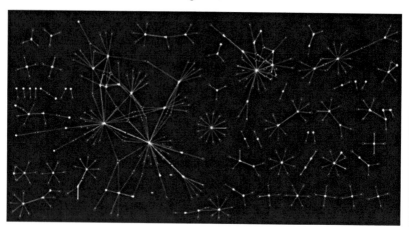

b) Recommendation network of a medical book

Product recommendation. Example of a Manga vs. a medical book

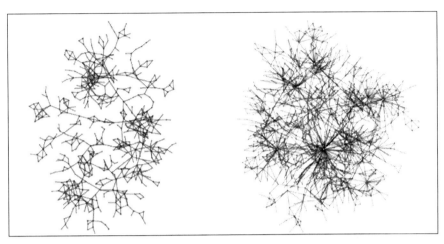

You can see the entire campaign in action from an interface as below (courtesy Xtract)

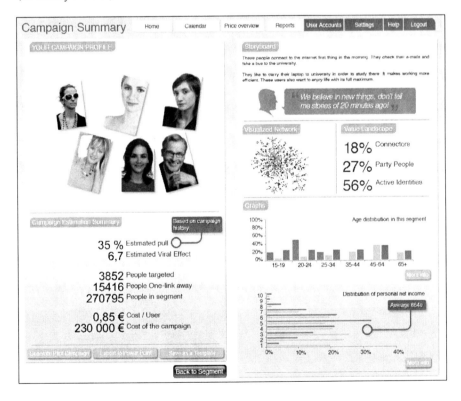

Audience exchanges: How metrics can improve advertiser efficiency

Companies such as Google and Yahoo are attempting to manage, organise and index information and content gathered from the Internet and the mobile Internet. The reason they are doing this is, to allow them to significantly increase their ability to target relevant commercial communications, to relevant audiences. Clearly, this is of interest and benefit to advertisers.

However, to achieve that goal a different approach is needed to understand and measure audiences. Today, most Internet and mobile advertising is managed by advertising networks and advertising exchanges, largely on a 'lowest-common-denominator, volume-driven basis. Given recent developments in how we are able to define and understand audiences, we see a new emerging business, best described as *Audience Exchanges*. Audience Exchanges are basically a way of enabling advertisers to find the most relevant and thus potentially valuable audience for their messages. As such they provide a bridge between social media platforms and networks, and advertisers.

An Audience Exchange is not a new idea or business. A similar notion, (albeit called a different name) has long existed within traditional media – with businesses established to deliver the benefits to users. For example, market research companies responsible for running the BARB TV panel in the UK provide the data and the analytics for media agencies to help their advertisers select the right audience for their campaigns.

Agencies use the raw BARB data (as an example) to build their own proprietary systems as an aid to plan the most efficient and effective mix of channels given the audience they are trying to reach and influence. There are also market research companies, and analytics businesses to provide software that do the same sort of thing. It is ironic that the Internet, for all its potential as a measured medium has to date not provided this sort of information to advertisers.

However as media forms evolve, and as we confront the reality of the networked society, such forms of rudimentary audience exchange, based as they are on sample data are quite simply inadequate. Today, people flow from media platform to media platform, from online and off, and on again, in what William Gibson described as 'blended reality'. As a consequence of that activity and behaviour, there is a real need for a new way of finding, selecting and defining groups of people that are interested in brands, products and services that could be of real use and relevance to them.

There is a key and important point to be made here. For many people, there is a growing alarm as to how much data is being collected and utilized for commercial purposes (headlines around 'The Big Brother Scenario', 'The Surveillance Culture' and so on). However, as Alan Moore has written, people need brands and brands need people. It's simply that today the techniques exist to help those brands and those people find each other, when they need each other the most.

Audience exchanges work between the media and the advertisers. They need data from various sources, and they enable media to deliver more revenue from advertising and marketing activities. Advertisers, media planners, and media buyers need audience exchanges to identify the right audience, be able to measure the impact of their activity and thus ultimately to deliver improved marketing results. To plan properly the agency needs access to a considerable amount of information and possess the right tools to make the most sense from what starts off as raw numbers, but soon becomes valuable, refined data. Examples of the data required include:

- Audience profiles to identify and size consumer segments
- Cross-media studies into the channels these segments are exposed to, and the channels they choose to consume
- Audience research into how best to reach and influence them
- Analysis tools to help explain how media forms work in combination, and
- Post-evaluation tools to help them measure the effect of their plan.

In the traditional media world this information is collected mainly from surveys, panels, and market research. In the case of social media, and social networks this information can be based on much more accurate individual levels of data. Although advertisers or agencies are not interested in individual data points, they need tools, profiles and metrics to find the right types of profile. This is important from a privacy point of view. The raw data must be refined. Different channels (e.g. social networking sites, mobile, and games) need similar methods to refine those data flows to create compatible profiles and metrics. It is essential to come up with a common method that enables brands to find the audiences they define as important to them in different channels; to use the same methodologies to measure results, and thus to allow planners to plan cross-media campaigns with confidence.

Not to do this will ignore the lessons of the past, when the failure of individual media forms to look beyond their own narrow interests limited the development of any true multi-media audience research tool, despite advertisers and agencies continuously highlighting the need for such an approach. Eventually the UK agencies, through their trade association, the IPA took the initiative and created the Touchpoints Study. The new, digital media forms need to learn from the debates, the arguments, the mistakes of the past, and understand the pressing need for a cross-media approach to audience analytics. Not to do so will unquestionably limit their revenue potential from advertisers.

Social media must make it easy for advertisers and agencies to buy and measure advertising. Common metrics and profiles are key components to making this happen.

Audience exchanges should be media or ad network independent. Some ad networks have attempted to develop their own audience exchange business, but this fragmented approach is not an effective model for themselves or for their advertisers. Agencies must be able to find the right target audience from different ad networks in the same way that today they are able to use(as an example) viewer profiles from different TV channels from a single, industry-accepted source. It is a benefit of all players in the ecosystem to have a common currency, providing consistent data across all social media and ad networks. It helps an ad network get on with the business of selling audiences for a better price, as opposed to spending time and money arguing over whose data is 'better'. Furthermore, a common currency helps social media forms find and justify a place on the agency's recommended plan.

The people best placed to drive the audience exchange idea forward are those analytics companies with the capability to process and refine

massive volumes (billions of gigabytes) of social media data. We predict that there will be several audience exchanges in the early phase of
their growth and they will no doubt develop different audience profiles
and metrics. However, for the reasons we've outlined above, we will see
consolidation in the business, and the development of de facto standards for identifying, and measuring audiences via an exchange model.

We have attempted to accelerate this process within this book by
presenting some guidelines and metrics to measure and profile audiences. Ajit is also working with these models in his Ph.D. work.

Audience exchanges still have several issues to solve:

- Where will profiles be generated from (which data points)?
- What ancillary data is necessary?
- What privacy guidelines will be required by statute law and by
  the industry itself?
- What logic will be used to create the right metrics?
- How will the data be kept fresh?
- What are the key benefits for people who offer their profile
  information?

All these issues can be tackled, when all key parties in the ecosystem accept that it is in their common interest to work together to
find compatible models that make it easier for advertisers and marketers
to utilize social media. The Internet world is traditionally dominated by
de facto standards and the first and fastest one often wins it all. The
telecom and mobile world is much more dominated by standards and
cooperation. We believe that we will see both approaches applied to

     Ajit Jaokar, Brian Jacobs, Alan Moore and Jouko Ahvenainen

the audience exchange business; it will be an interesting competition between different approaches.

Audience exchanges will help drive advertising and marketing initiatives within the social media. Mobile and social media data can provide important market research and audience information to all companies involved in media and advertising. Mobile or social media can be a crucial element within a cross-media campaign, be it as a feedback channel for mass media campaigns, or as an engagement component within campaigns (as in Barack Obama's campaign for the US Presidency). They can be also be used as a pure market research source, for example for providing information on social network activity helping users understand what kind of people spend time in undertaking different types of activity.

A natural next step for Audience Exchanges is to give more control and power to the consumer, as the ultimate end-user. In the future, consumers will further be able to manage and utilize their own digital footprint and profile. Certainly they can use this data to ensure that they receive information on products and services of relevance to them, but ultimately this concept will expand, and consumers will be able to go further, to manage their daily tasks, a bit like having a personal assistant in mobile or on the internet. There are already projects like CRM 2.0 and VRM (Vendor Relationship Management) that are developing in this direction; some of Amazon's services are similar.

All this is still at a very early phase, but we predict that the development of services and tools around the notion of consumer control of his/her own data will be the next big thing, not only in social marketing intelligence, but across every aspect of the management of customer relationships. Consumers will be more in control of their own data, which will (amongst other things) lead to them having more power over how they receive communications from, and how they interact with brands.

 Ajit Jaokar, Brian Jacobs, Alan Moore and Jouko Ahvenainen

Privacy

The significance of privacy

We have discussed social media marketing from the perspective of social networks,telecoms and media. We have also seen that the underlying data is the glue that binds these platforms together. Data and privacy/ trust are two sides of the same coin. Advertisers need data to make their advertising more personalised (and by extension, to improve their return-on-investment), but the acquisition of the data means that the customer often gives up his privacy rights in the interests of the advertiser.

Thus, data and privacy are two sides of the same coin. Hence, we can view privacy as a key perspective within social media marketing alongside data.

Most marketers are very aware of the privacy concerns of their customers and with a few well-publicised exceptions, most adhere to statutory regulations. However, with the rapid growth of social media and mobility, the industry as a whole is beginning to encounter new issues and we believe that higher standards are needed beyond the statutory minimum. Consequently, we approach the topic of privacy below with this mindset of 'beyond the statutory minimum'

Most countries have laws pertaining to data protection. In the

UK, we have the Data Protection Act [84] which is an Act of Parliament. This defines a legal basis for handling information relating to people living within the UK. Although the Act does not mention privacy, in practice it provides a way in which individuals can enforce the control of information about themselves. Organisations in the UK are legally obliged to comply with this Act, subject to some exemptions.

Social networks and mobile bring new challenges as we demonstrate below. For instance, the mobile is a personal device. Unlike a PC or a Web connection, it is not shared. Hence, we need regulation to protect individuals especially the more vulnerable – for example children. Mobile providers and operators already adhere to many existing rules and safeguards – for instance they have Opt-in and Double Opt-in (where a secondary confirmation is needed – for example, an email).

So, we have to ask ourselves:

a) Do we need guidelines/higher standards beyond the statutory measures?

b) Do we need measures specific to mobile and to social networks? (As opposed to purely online)

The need for higher standards beyond a statutory minimum

We show below why privacy issues are a genuine concern and why a higher standard is needed going forward. We believe that engendering trust can also be genuinely beneficial to the providers.

Cutting edge advances in communication technology, the 'art of the

84   http://en.wikipedia.org/wiki/Data_Protection_Act

possible' is not always in the interest of the customer. We have seen a lot of advances in mobile and Web technology in recent years, and certainly the aim of those who have invested in these new technologies is to recoup at least a part of their investment from brand-supported activities. The interests of marketers are not necessarily aligned with the interests of the customer. Hence, the notion that 'Customers need brands and brands need customers' has to be tempered with the basic reality that the primary purpose of brands is to sell. As media becomes rich and complex, brands seek to engage with us and to measure that engagement in order to maximise their revenue. Within this new communication world, a balancing force is needed to look after the interests of the customer. This relates especially to the issue of privacy.

As we indicated before, data and privacy/trust are two sides of the same coin. Advertisers need data to make their advertising more personalised; acquiring this data can compromise the individual's right to privacy

Consider the emphasis on 'Convergence'. If the media and advertisers were indeed able to 'join the dots' between the various information elements left by us, the cookie crumbs of information left lying around often without our knowledge in different media, then advertising has the potential to become more personalised, more relevant, more effective. This benefits the advertiser, and the media owner especially in a converged media scenario (where the same provider owns the TV, landline, mobile subscriptions etc) – but at the same time could lead to an abuse of data (even if technically a legal abuse of data), and to a consumer backlash (which of course helps no-one).

Consider the following scenario:

Suppose a person mentions in their blog that they are a fan of a certain rock group. . Now also consider that many TV companies are exploring ways to 'personalise' TV advertising to the home. For instance, they seek to gain viewing preferences from set top boxes and other avenues and then (in an extreme scenario), to tailor the advertising to each home. This means less wasteful marketing for the advertiser, and more relevant, and potentially more useful brand communications for the viewer.

The question is: Which data elements can be used to tailor this advertising?

Consider the 'rock group' data element which can be obtained from an RSS feed from the blog. Now it is easy to combine three sets of data: The home address and the person's name which the cable company has along with the RSS feed from their blog (which ties to the person's name) and the phone book/voter registration (as a confirmation of the address).

Knowing these elements, the cable TV company can in theory then 'personalise' the advertisement to the viewer, in other words to screen an advertisement for the group's next concert. The viewer can also be offered a chance to pay to view a forthcoming televised concert by the band.

This is good for the advertiser, and it could be argued good for the viewer, who may otherwise remain unaware of his favourite band's forthcoming appearances. On the other hand, others might argue that this is a gross invasion of privacy and questionable 'Big Brother' tactics, as the viewer did not specifically agree to be 'sold to' in this way. The use to which data is put is likely to grow, as the technology supporting it becomes more widespread. The danger is that data elements from different data sets will be used without our knowing it to gain new insights about us, which can then be used to 'sell' to us.

We could call this 'Micropersuasion' and indeed it raises questions about the ethics of how data is used to communicate with us, to market to us, to govern us (although none of this behaviour would be seen to be illegal). Such a use of data could also raise the spectre of a consumer backlash against those using data in this way.

Governments – often part of the problem

While advertisers will inevitably push the envelope when it comes to using data to aid the targeting of their messages, sometimes even at the expense of privacy, in some cases Governments have also followed suit. Governments are supposed to be a part of the solution – but in some cases they are a part of the problem.

Governments need to be involved in two ways: First, in the creation of regulation that benefits consumers in addition to the advertisers especially in relation to new areas where regulation is sparse and consumers can be potentially exploited. Secondly, in ensuring that the privacy rights of individuals are protected in the light of ever increasing encroachments from brands and advertisers.

At one level, we have laws such as the data protection laws in the UK. However, at another level, governments can be a part of the problem; an example would be the proposed law on 'Data Sharing' in the UK.

Under the guise of 'mass exchange of data can offer some benefits', the UK Government is proposing legislation[85] (source the Telegraph web

---

85   http://www.telegraph.co.uk/news/newstopics/politics/4339771/Threat-to-privacy-under-data-law-

site) *where data held by the police, the NHS, schools, the Inland Revenue, local councils and the DVLA could all end up in private hands, according to Privacy International. At the same time, information gathered by companies including hotel registrations, bank details and telecommunications data could be transferred to the Government as part of the provisions of the Coroner's and Justice Bill, it is claimed. The campaign group admits the "mass exchange of personal information has the potential to deliver some benefit".*

The net impact of a lack of trust in the Government is customers will trust no one! Leading to a stalemate which benefits no-one.

Targeting minorities and ethnic groups

Another grey area is targeting minorities and ethnic groups. Legally, there is no law that prevents the targeting of specific ethnic groups by advertisers. In fact, it can be profitable to do so as per the benefits from the ad network JumpTap which predicted that Hispanic-centric campaigns[86] would quadruple this year, with revenue increasing at least 20% in the sector.

Of course, there is nothing wrong in selling Hispanic oriented content, music, food, drinks, clothing, cosmetics targeting a specific demographic – but change the model slightly and you get some serious privacy concerns. For instance, the South Asian population is genetically susceptible to diabetes[87].

Does this mean that diabetes medication advertisements should be targeted to South Asians in the UK?

---

campaigners-warn.html
86 http://adage.com/digital/article?article_id=134036
87 http://news.bbc.co.uk/1/hi/health/7760413.stm

Again, this is not too difficult to do using current technology and increasing convergence and data availability. But a simple approach, sending an inevitably common message to large groups, could cause problems. The South Asian population is not a homogeneous group; there are different groups who are susceptible in different ways to different strains of diabetes. In this case, using data without the knowledge and permission of the individuals to whom the data refers could lead to incorrect advice being transmitted, and received by potentially vulnerable individuals.

Where do we draw the line?

In the USA, drug companies are allowed to advertise medication direct-to-consumers on television. This is illegal in many countries – including Europe. The message from these DTC advertisements can be summarised as: *'Call your General practitioner(GP) and ask him to prescribe you our drugs'*.

Broadcasting drug company advertisements on television raises two ethical issues. First, it encourages self-diagnosis, which may not be the right thing for the patient medically. Second, it pressurises the doctor to suggest certain branded drugs over other alternatives – as the customer thinks he knows what's best for him based on what he has seen on the TV.Hence, in many countries, this form of advertising is illegal.

Pushing the boundaries – consumer kids

Yet another area is protection of minors especially in an era dominated by mobile and social networking.

Social networks, mobile and other emerging mediums offer the possibility of targeting commercial messages to children. Again, this practise is not illegal but based on how regulators have stepped in to limit traditional media advertising to children some consider it to be morally questionable.

As per the Guardian[88], *the book 'Consumer Kids' introduces a case study: seven-year-old Sarah, who has been recruited through Dubit.com to act as a brand ambassador for Mattel and promote her Barbie MP3 player to school friends. In exchange for keeping the sought-after shiny pink gadget, her job description includes creating a fansite where she blogs about the product, taking pictures of her sales missions and posting them back to Dubit, where she is rewarded.*

Impulse purchasing

As more and more mobile devices are able to be used to purchase goods and services, extending the above discussion, we enter into the realm of the ethics of impulse purchasing. Impulse purchasing is not unethical in itself. Supermarkets for instance regularly encourage impulse purchases though such as using aisle-ends, bins and placing items such as confectionary close to the tills.

However, with mobile devices, new problems could arise.

Consider the example of the phone 'reminding' you to buy a related product. This would be based on 'opt-in' so it's not SPAM. So far, so good. At worst a minor irritation – at best a useful recommendation.

Now extend this further. Knowing the person, object they are looking at (based on location – for example they are standing in front of a car show room) and their credit history (available on the Web), can we 'sell' a 'One click' loan? – to 'engage' with the person and 'encourage'

---

88   http://www.guardian.co.uk/media/2009/jan/26/marketing-online-children-kids-underage-regulation

---

them to buy the car?

Legally and technologically this is not illegal; indeed TV companies screen supposedly cheap loan ads at times of the day when the most vulnerable are likely to be viewing. However, morally and ethically it is at least dubious (depending on whether the person is already in debt). Note that all this precise engagement and personalization can be enabled by co-relating different datasets.

Profiles – individual vs. anonymised

The question of profiles is also interesting and raises some questions.

For instance consider the abstract of the following patent filed by Google (source search engine journal)[89]

Results based personalization of advertisements in a search engine, was filed yesterday by Google and is described in the abstract as: Personalized advertisements are provided to a user using a search engine to obtain documents relevant to a search query. The advertisements are personalized in response to a search profile that is derived from personalized search results. The search results are personalized based on a user profile of the user providing the query. The user profile describes interests of the user, and can be derived from a variety of sources, including prior search queries, prior search results, expressed interests, demographic, geographic, psychographic, and activity information.

Such a profile would appear to be recording all our activities in cyberspace and tying them individually to specific individuals (to be used for the purposes of advertising). This practise does raise privacy concerns

---

89   http://www.searchenginejournal.com/google-advertising-patents-for-behavioral-targeting-personalization-and-profiling/2311/

On the other side are anonymised profiles which seek to anonymise personal data and then create 'templates' of user behaviour which may be used to predict future behaviour based on past behaviour. For instance, it may be used to identify in advance who will churn from a social network. In this case, rather than getting an individual profile, we get audience segments. Audience segments are not tied to individuals (of course in a very small segment – for example a segment of one – they could be).

Consequently the definition, meaning and usage of profiles is not clear and more awareness , transparency and user education is needed.

Special considerations for mobile

The mobile operators generally have a good reputation for managing data and preventing misuse from advertisers. Misleading promotions like Crazy Frog ringtone[90] in the UK were not created by telecom operators but rather by mobile marketing companies. In the case of the Crazy Frog ringtone, children had been duped into signing up for expensive subscription services.

Certainly, most operators take privacy seriously and as a whole the mobile ecosystem has not been plagued by malware and advertising malpractices as has media and the Web.

Over time, operators and the industry will face new challenges as they start to work with new forms of advertising as we have indicated in the discussion above. Whatever the direction we choose, we believe that 'mobile' due to its unique, personalised nature will have to go beyond 'Opt-in' and may need higher standards beyond statutory regulation based on moral and ethical integrity in order to protect consumer interests.

---

90   http://www.out-law.com/page-5862

Mobile as a tool for psychosocial development and identity formation

The injecting of branding messages to personalised platforms like mobile devices (and also social networks) is significant because mobile impacts the psychosocial development of youth[91]. . By psychosocial development, we mean that the mobile device is more than a communicative medium but is also a means of shaping Identity for the youth as discussed in the MIT Press/Mc Arthur foundation paper 'Mobile Identity: Youth, Identity, and Mobile Communication Media' by Gitte Stald[92]

The value of the mobile depends on contextual uses and experiences which makes the mobile device a key social artefact in the minds of the young[93]. In contrast, the industry has approached the idea of Mobile Youth in terms of brands, marketing, engagement etc and not really in terms of the impact of the phone on the creation of identity and the social development of young people.

The paper Mobile Identity: Youth, Identity, and Mobile Communication Media concludes:

In the context of this article, however, I have focused primarily on the social meanings of the mobile. As we have seen, the mobile supports and enhances the maintenance of social groups and the feeling of belonging to a group. Young people live in a period of time--historically as well as in terms of age--which is characterized by a collectively and personally perceived sense of fragmentation and uncertainty. Many social theorists have argued that traditional resources for identity formation are no longer so easily available,

91 http://en.wikipedia.org/wiki/Psychosocial_development
92 http://www.mitpressjournals.org/toc/dmal/-/6?cookieSet=1
93 http://cenriqueortiz.com/pubs/themobilecontext/TheMobileContext-CEnriqueOrtiz.pdf

and that the realization of personal expectations for "the good life" may seem increasingly difficult. Young people also have to deal with the sometimes conflicting expectations of parents, school, and friends. Social networks--the strong ties as well as the weak, ephemeral relations--offer possibilities for testing oneself in the light of shared values, norms and codes, for negotiating collective and personal identity, and for establishing a sense of belonging. The mobile is the glue that holds together various nodes in these social networks: it serves as the predominant personal tool for the coordination of everyday life, for updating oneself on social relations, and for the collective sharing of experiences. It is therefore the mediator of meanings and emotions that may be extremely important in the ongoing formation of young people's identities.

The need to learn how to manage and to develop personal identity and the importance of social networks in this process are strongly facilitated by mobiles; and this makes it possible to talk about "mobile identity." The constant negotiation of values and representations and the need to identify with others result in a fluidity of identity which goes beyond the ongoing process of identity formation, to encompass the constant negotiation of norms and values and the processes of reflection that are characteristic of contemporary social life.

The constant availability and presence associated with the mobile demonstrate how important it has become in all these arenas, even to those who use it only moderately. The mobile enforces an increasingly intense pace of communication and of intellectual and emotional experience. It, therefore, becomes both the cause and the

   Ajit Jaokar, Brian Jacobs, Alan Moore and Jouko Ahvenainen

potential solution to the frustrations of young people regarding the potential management of everyday life. The mobile is an important tool that allows one to be in control--which is an essential ability for adolescents in general--but simultaneously it is becoming more and more important to be able to control the mobile.

Since the mobile is the primary means of learning, social interaction, identity formation etc amongst young people – and it is an individual, personalised device – the question is – To what extent should brand marketing, and external communications in general influence the minds of people – especially the young?

Methods to empower the user – the future of privacy

As we demonstrate in the above examples, many new factors will come into play and industry, customers and the regulators will face new challenges. We believe that ultimately, the solution lies in empowering the user. In this section, we discuss the methods by which this could be achieved. As we have discussed before, enlightened and empowered users will ultimately trust the providers and will be loyal customers (hence good for business).

Full disclosure

As we have discussed before, disclosure and transparency will add to customer loyalty. Transparency is a complicated issue especially as technology gets more complex. However, certainly an attempt needs to be made to educate the user in how best to manage his or her own data, and the implications of revealing this data to external organisations of any hue.

Vrm – vendor relationship management

There are emerging initiatives that empower the customer. One such initiative is Vendor Relationship Management at Harvard Law School[94]. According to their site:

VRM, or Vendor Relationship Management, is the reciprocal of CRM or Customer Relationship Management. It provides customers with tools for engaging with vendors in ways that work for both parties.

CRM systems for the duration have borne the full burden of relating with customers. VRM will provide customers with the means to bear some of that weight, and to help make markets work for both vendors and customers ó in ways that don't require the former to "lock in" the latter.

The goal of VRM is to improve the relationship between Demand and Supply by providing new and better ways for the former to relate to the latter. In a larger sense, VRM immodestly intends to improve markets and their mechanisms by equipping customers to be independent leaders and not just captive followers in their relationships with vendors and other parties on the supply side of the marketplace.

For VRM to work, vendors must have reason to value it, and customers must have reasons to invest the necessary time, effort and attention to making it work. Providing those reasons to both sides is the primary challenge for VRM.

94   http://cyber.law.harvard.edu/projectvrm/Main_Page

VRM principles include:

- Relationships are voluntary.
- Customers are born free and independent of vendors.
- Customers control their own data. They can share data selectively and control the terms of its use.
- Customers are points of integration and origination for their own data.
- Customers can assert their own terms of engagement and service.
- Customers are free to express their demands and intentions outside any company's control.

We expect that there will be other initiatives that will arise similar to VRM with the goal of empowering the end user.

Anonymity

Increasingly we will see the emergence of many mechanisms that anonymise data at the source with the user's permission. User managed anonymity could provide both safety and could help create a business model based on trust.

Web 2.0 has taught us the concept of harnessing collective intelligence. Companies like Google with Page Rank, Amazon (with Amazon Reviews) and others have benefited from the idea of harnessing collective intelligence. So, the business model for the provider in harnessing collective intelligence is proven. Creators of data own the copyright to the individual data elements (for instance reviews of books) but the providers own the value gained from harnessing that granular data. Providers of services would postulate that the granular data elements don't hold commercial value – it is only the aggregated elements (harnessing collective intelligence) that have value.

Or does it?

In other words, is there any value in the granular data as opposed to the aggregated data?

Let us put this in perspective.

Currently, providers can (largely) provide personalised services and some form of targeted advertising and also segmentation. That does not need customers to 'own' their own data.

The question arises, Is there a model which would enable both providers and customers to benefit if data is owned and managed by the customers themselves?

To explain this issue, we have to understand the problem of k-anonymity. The problem and solution of k-anonymity relates to re-identifying individuals from multiple datasets even if the data is (supposedly) anonymised. As we become creators of data with Web 2.0 (and Mobile Web 2.0), the problem becomes significant because data is collected by providers at a phenomenal rate. It is then possible in theory to re-identify people from datasets.

This discussion explores the possibility of making the problem of anonymization into a business opportunity. Essentially, if data is anonymised at the source and is under the control of the customer, the customer will trust the provider who anonymises their data. In return for that trust, the customer could volunteer to reveal attributes about themselves which would enable the provider to create personalized communication campaigns and also to be used in segmentation. This benefits both the providers (protection from legal action, personalized advertising, segmentation) and also the customers (anonymised data, personalised services etc).

To elaborate this idea further, we consider the example of k-anonymity. The concept of k-anonymity is summarised in a paper by Latanya Sweeney – 'K-Anonymity: A Model For Protecting Privacy' School of Computer Science, Carnegie Mellon University, Pittsburgh, Pennsylvania, USA as per the paper abstract[95]

Consider a data holder, such as a hospital or a bank, that has a privately held collection of person-specific, field structured data. Suppose the data holder wants to share a version of the data with researchers. How can a data holder release a version of its private data with scientific guarantees that the individuals who are the subjects of the data cannot be re-identified while the data remain practically useful? The solution provided in this paper includes a formal protection model named k-anonymity and a set of accompanying policies for deployment. A release provides k-anonymity protection if the information for each person contained in the release cannot be distinguished from at least k-1 individuals whose information also appears in the release. This paper also examines re-identification attacks that can be realized on releases that adhere to kanonymity unless accompanying policies are respected. The k-anonymity protection model is important because it forms the basis on which the real-world systems known as Datafly, – Argus and k-Similar provide guarantees of privacy protection.

Keywords: data anonymity, data privacy, re-identification, data fusion, privacy.

---

95 Full paper : http://privacy.cs.cmu.edu/people/sweeney/kanonymity.pdf

The basic problem applies to all data. Historically, data has been anonymised by removing explicit identifiers such as name, address, telephone number etc. Such data looks anonymised but it may not be when co-related with another dataset which may help to uniquely identify people.

For example, as per the paper, in Massachusetts, the Group Insurance Commission (GIC) is responsible for purchasing health insurance for state employees. Because the data were believed to be anonymous, GIC gave a copy of the data to researchers and sold a copy to industry. It was then possible to co-relate it with normal voter registration. This information can be linked using ZIP code, birth date and gender to the medical information, thereby linking diagnosis, procedures, and medications to particularly named individuals. For example, William Weld was governor of Massachusetts at that time and his medical records were in the GIC data. Governor Weld lived in Cambridge Massachusetts. According to the Cambridge Voter list, six people had his particular birth date; only three of them were men; and, he was the only one in his 5-digit ZIP code.

The solution for this problem is the creation of a policy managed by the user which anonymises data (perhaps at the source itself).

From a mobile perspective, the policy manager should be designed to:

a) Be controlled by the user. The user sets the policies
b) Manage all data – not just location

This is a potentially win-win situation because essentially, if data is anonymised at the source and is under the control of the customer, the

Copyright © Futuretext Ltd   Ajit Jaokar, Brian Jacobs, Alan Moore and Jouko Ahvenainen customer will trust the provider who anonymises their data (and in turn protects them).

The approach potentially provides a compelling argument for both the provider and the customer. In doing so, it is different from current approaches because at the moment, advertising, segmentation etc can be implemented on a best case basis (i.e. without knowing the exact data from the customer) – but a trust based approach will benefit all parties through accurate personalization but will be managed by the user.

Revocation

Conventional privacy models lean towards a closed, digital fortress. These can take many forms – LinkedIn introductions, signed applications, third party trust endorsers, and so on. In turn, conventional revocation models are provider driven ex – certificate removal of malicious applications. The current methods don't fit the current open web ecosystem and more importantly a future web based ecosystem where there is a tendency to give up privacy with a younger generation.

It could be possible to consider a user driven revocation model.

Social networks are increasingly going to be the primary form of interface to the Web for many of us. Unlike the Open Web, the social network has some form of structure (profiles, messages etc). In this scenario, within the social web, privacy and revocation could go side by side creating a new privacy model. In other words, the user will be open to contact but in return – he or she will choose to exercise the right to terminate that contact if they need to. This model is based on 'innocent until proven guilty' as opposed to the existing digital fortress ecosystem (guilty until proven innocent)

Admittedly, the revocation engine may not work in context of the whole web but it may well work in context of a social network. Currently, the spam features within Gmail work in a similar way (except Google does the revocation implicitly on our behalf)

The model is a switch on existing privacy models. It strengthens the revocation – not the moat bridge; let people cross the moat freely, but always allow them the revocation engine as a defence mechanism.

Conclusions

Data and privacy go together. For marketers, the temptation to treat social media as a 'channel' is strong, along with the desire to retrofit the new world of communication to the familiar world of brands, traffic, audiences, growth etc. However, this is not always in the consumer's interest.

We believe that social networks and mobile, due to their unique, personalised nature will have to go beyond 'Opt-in' and may need higher standards beyond statutory regulation based on moral and ethical integrity in order to protect consumer interests.

Historically, consumers have not always liked advertising but most accept advertising and we all benefit from it. New technologies will mean that advertising will be more personalised but in doing so, the user's identity should always be protected. The future lies in empowering the customer and building relationships based on genuine trust, openness and transparency. Ultimately, such relationships will be profitable to both providers and brands.

Data and privacy form the bedrock of this multi-way conversation between the marketer and the participants. Ultimately, we see the participants and the marketer enter into a trusted relationship based on transparency where the participants share data about themselves and entrust the marketer with their data in return for a better and more personalised service.

Case studies

This section gives a set of case studies to illustrate the concepts we have discussed so far.

Social marketing intelligence applied to churn

The Customer

In a mature market where mobile penetration rates can be up to 130%+, churn management becomes an essential activity for the CMO. The CMO has previously used churn scoring by modeling churners with traditional data mining tools.

The Challenge

The operator/CMO needs to increase the retention of existing customers by deploying more effective churn management by utilizing new tools that offer a superior capability. The issue is not only to target churn campaigns, but more importantly how to make the right level of investments in each potential churner class.

The Solution

The operator deploys *social network and behavior analytics* to improve the results of churn scoring. The operator can identify subscribers that have the highest risk to churn, and also potential churners that have the highest influence on their social circle, i.e. they would take their friends or family members with them to another operator.

The operator is also able to calculate the social revenue of each subscriber. Social Revenue means the aggregated revenue of a subscriber and his or her social circle. Churn is viral. Social Revenue is an important new factor to evaluate the value of subscribers, because it enables operators to understand the total value of individuals. For example, there can be a subscriber who is the central hub in his social circle, e.g. in a family, but he doesn't make many calls, but other people call him. If he takes another operator, his contacts can follow him, and the operator loses the revenue of all these subscribers.

The operator is now in a position to know subscribers who are [1] high churn risk [2] people who have high influence on other potential churners, [3] the social revenue of each subscriber. The operator can also profile subscribers and their usage within a social context.

Now the operator can allocate the appropriate resources to churn management activities targeting the right people and also tailor the right message for each target. The operator can, for example, give a special gift or offer to the most important targets, e.g. 2% of the most important churn Alpha Users. The gift or offer can be selected based on a subscriber's profile. For a gadget freak young man it could be the latest mobile phone model, for a culturally inclined woman, it could be a concert ticket, or for a budget limited phone heavy user it could be an extra discount. For the next 3% percent of churn Alpha Users, the operator can make outbound calls to find if they have any issues with their subscription, or if they would like to take another package. And for the next 5%

of the most important Alpha Users the operator can send a letter to provide more information on available services and packages.

The Results

The operator is able to allocate its churn management resources in an optimal way.

Results from clients provide significant bottom line results from this kind of analytics and marketing activities:

- Churn in the Alpha communities decreased more than in traditional targeting groups and this brought an estimated annual 6.25 percent improvement for the operator's revenue.
- Using CDR and social network analysis in addition to demographic data, produces (in this case) a 21% increase in predicting churn than a corresponding regression model based on demographic information only. For one operator that resulted in a saving of 40m for one financial year.
- The top 5% of churn Alpha Users have a 8 times higher influence in their social circle when they churn than subscribers that were not Alpha Users, i.e. if any of these important Alpha Users churned, they took 8 times more friends, family members, or colleagues with them than non Alpha Users.

Social marketing intelligence applied to launch of new services

The Customer

A Mobile Operator is launching a new mobile email service. The operator has over 30M subscribers.

The Challenge

The penetration of services within this particular market is growing rapidly. However, suddenly growth stops. The operator has about 50,000 users for an email service. The same has happened earlier also with other services. The operator begins to analyze the reasons for the phenomena. By analyzing the customer data, the operator can identify that growth stops when early adopters have taken up the service. Early adopters are interested in trying all new services, and also services that are more difficult to install and use.

Early adopters are often a special group that has no influence on other users. And their feedback doesn't necessary help to spread the service to other users.

The Solution

The operator starts to use social network and behavior analytics to improve the results of product launches. The operator can identify subscribers that have a high propensity to start using a new service, and also potential users that have the highest influence on their social circle, i.e. these subscribers have a high Alpha score.

The operator decides to activate Alpha Users in a marketing

campaign. The traditional and easy way to do this is to offer something like special discounts or gifts for subscribers who are able to attract their friends to take up a new service. But often, people are not willing to promote products to their friends, especially if they believe they are part of an advertising spamming campaign. But people are willing to pass on and importantly advocate those services or products, that enable them to achieve higher status and respect within their peer group, or share something that is perceived as valuable information or entertainment to that peer group. This means, for example, exclusive offers that can be shared with friends, information concerning new products and services, or games and competitions where people can play and compete with other people and get recognition if they are successful. In this case, it is a premium email package, that includes a special price flat rate data package.

The network effect is important in services like mobile email. Users get more value from it, when their friends and colleagues also use it. So, it is not only to find Alpha Users, but communities where the operator has many potential users and can target marketing specifically to these communities first.

The operator also collects feedback from Alpha Users to improve the service and its usability. The most important Alpha Users are invited to focus groups.

The Results

The operator is able to achieve a break through not only with the email service, but also with other new advanced services. The amount of users starts to grow beyond the old 50,000 limit. The operator finds that growth of 500,000 to one million users for services that were not successful earlier, not uncommon. And the operator receives a great deal of valuable feedback to further develop these services.

Social marketing intelligence used to launch ring back tone service

The Customer
The operator has over 5M subscribers and is launching the ring back tone service.

The Challenge
The operator needs new products to increase ARPU, especially when competition pushes prices down. But it seems to be difficult to get customers to take to value-added-services.

To make matters even more challenging, the penetration of services is growing slowly or indeed the growth stops again with early adopters. The operator spends heavily on traditional media marketing, utilising magazine and outdoor marketing campaigns, without a great deal of success. The product managers would like to attach marketing material to telephone bills, but many other product managers would also like to get their product material with the bills. So there is an organisational stalemate on how to best proceed.

The Solution
The operator decides to utilise social network and behavior analytics to improve the results of the product launches. In this case, the operator

deploys behavior and social network analytics separately. The operator uses social networking data (CDR's from calls and text messages), usage data (those who are already using the service, those who use some similar music services, and those who normally adopt a new service in an early phase of launch), combined with demographical data. These separate information flows are fed into an automated social marketing intelligence tool that has a powerful analytics engine that takes those separate data flows and begins to look for patterns and intelligence that otherwise would remain hidden.

Intentionally, the operator wants to keep behavior and social network scoring separate, i.e. the operator does not combine a pure Alpha score with propensity scores to get Product Marketing Alpha scores. A part of the marketing is targeted at subscribers with the highest propensity scores (Propensity Group) and another part to subscribers with the highest Alpha Score (Alpha Group).

With the results of the Social Marketing Intelligence outputs, the operator was able to make a direct marketing pitch to a highly targeted and selected groups.

The Results
- The direct pull (i.e. how many subscribers who were in the target group decided to take up the product) in the behavior Propensity Group was 19.8%.
- The direct pull in the Alpha Group was 12.7%. So, it was lower than in the propensity target group.
- But the operator also measured the indirect pull, i.e. how many neighbors of the target group adopts the service. In the

propensity group, the total viral effect (how many neighbors of the service users take the service) was 1.14%, when in the Alpha group it was 2.16%. This means, the viral effect was approximately 90% higher in the Alpha group.

- This case clearly demonstrates that optimum results are achieved by combining all three dimensions of data (demographics, behavior, and social network) and by combining propensity and social network scoring results with each other. In this way, target groups are selected that possess the highest probability to adopt a product and also have high viral influence within social networks.

Social marketing intelligence for magazine publishing

The Customer

A Magazine publications community web site for teenagers.

The Objectives

- To gain a better understanding of the people in the community
- To attract more subscribers of the Magazine to the community platform
- To add new Magazine subscribers from the online subscriber and visitor base
- To gain greater knowledge and insight of active users and influencers so as to develop the content of the web site and the Magazine
- To make the community profitable by utilizing online information for marketing to the advertisers

The Solution

- Phase 1: The publisher identified the most influential users of the community, the Alpha Users, using advanced social network analytics. These were 2% of the online subscriber base.
- Phase 2: The publisher identified 9 community segments based on the online and demographic data of the Magazine subscribers. It also created specific profiles of the complete subscriber base.

The Results

- With accurate and current customer profiles the Magazine was able to target the segments better and be more effective in the marketing campaigns for the Magazine. The publisher achieved an estimated 3.8 times increase in revenues when Alphas were engaged in community marketing.
- Involvement of the Alpha Users in focus groups, and engaging them in creating content and actively promoting the publication in the communities around them, led the Chief Editor receiving up-to-date, fact based information from users, to follow the postings of identified Alpha Users.
- The community as a social network was analysed, which identified nine Web communities based on online and demographic data of the Magazine subscribers. Specific profiles of the entire subscriber base were created. In doing so, there was a 3.8 times increase in revenues when hubs participated in viral commercial communication activity.

- By knowing the profiles of the users, the Magazine was able to also improve -o their banner advertising with higher response rates. Advertisers and media agencies were able to demonstrate improved advertising response rates, as they could access user profiles for media selection. Advertisers were also ready to pay higher advertising prices as they could knowingly target their advertising to the most relevant segments.
- Customer understanding and profiles also helped the company to develop improved and more relevant content for the Magazine and the community platform. By using social network intelligence segments it was possible to develop specific segments and content categories for their printed and on-line content, fulfilling the needs of all main community segments.

Social marketing intelligence for broadcasting

The Customer
A TV production and broadcasting company. The company has a main community that consists of several TV series sub-communities. In these communities, users can have a discussion with other users, post comments to discussion forums, and look for and buy content.

The Objectives
- To profile the people using the website in order to have better customer insight for internal content development and offer better information to third parties including advertisers.

 Ajit Jaokar, Brian Jacobs, Alan Moore and Jouko Ahvenainen

- To profile people who are active in each TV series' sub-community, and Alpha Users of each community in order to find users preferences and interests to better utilize them in development, focus groups, and word-of-mouth marketing.
- To make the web site profitable by utilizing online information for marketing to advertisers.

The Solution

The rich profiling created from user behaviour and social context included the following information:

1) How different sub-communities are linked to each from usage point-of-view,
2) User profiles each sub-community,
3) Usage and content profile for each sub-community,
4) Alpha User profiles,
5) Profiles for other user groups: loyal, occasional, and passerby users, and
6) Buzz and engagement scores in each user group and sub-community.

The ability to automate the harvesting and refining of this intelligence, provided constant up-to-date information that allowed the close monitoring of the unfolding memes, changes and trends in the community.

The Results

A solution was implemented using which the broadcaster was able to capture all the profile and social network information available. The broadcaster utilised the Social Intelligence first for its own internal needs and also to develop content. Alpha User information was a crucial component of the solution. The broadcaster was also able follow the opinions of the Alpha Users and be more sensitive to their opinions than to other average users. The broadcaster was also able to invite the top Alpha Users to focus groups and panels where they could participate in the development of the on-line service, especially in the TV show offering and content.

At the moment, the company is planning next steps such as enriched profiles for TV advertisers, and the ability to make more targeted offers to the community of advertisers..

Social marketing intelligence applied to reducing churn for telecoms operators

A mobile operator has 31 million subscribers. Their annual churn rate is 24%, i.e. they lose approximately 7.4 million subscribers a year. Their ARPU (average revenue per user) is 45 euro a month. This means that they lose over 4 billion euro revenue due to churners.

In this example we illustrate the viral influence in churn. In order to simplify the example, we have made some assumptions based on real customer case data. We assume that 4% subscribers are top level Alpha Users (Alpha1), i.e. they have 20% viral effect in churn. This means, that if any of these Alpha1's churn, 20% of their neighbors also churn. We also assume that 15% of subscribers are lower level influencers (Alpha2). If any of these Alpha2's churn, 10% of their neighbors also churn. We assume (again based on real cases) that the churn influence of all other subscribers is 3%.

In this example, each Alpha1 has average 6.0 neighbors over whom they have direct influence in their social network. Similarly Alpha2 has 4.5 neighbors and other subscribers 1.5 neighbors. We can now calculate that the average viral effect of churn is 18.9%. So, in total 1.2M subscribers churn due to the viral effect.

When we know higher influencers (Alpha1 and Alpha2), we can focus the churn management activities to these subscribers and stop the viral churn effectively. In this example, we are able to stop 28% of the Alpha1 churn and 12% of Alpha2 churn. In this way we can prevent 155,691 subscribers from churning. This means 84M euro more revenue for the operator annually.

In this example, we only calculate the viral effect of the churn. Social network analysis also improves the accuracy of churn scoring for individuals, when social neighborhood is a factor that predicts an individual's churn propensity. So, the total value of social network based churn scoring is higher than the viral influence alone, or more than 84M euro in additional revenue.

The calculations are as overleaf.

		Editable cells				
Number of customers	31,000,000					
Number of Alpha1 Users	1,240,000					
Number of Alpha2 Users	4,650,000					
Number of Normal Users	25,110,000					
Current churn rate	24%					
Number of churners	7,440,000					
ARPU	€45					
Lost revenue	€4,017,600,000					
Average viral effect	0.189					
Original churners	6,257,247					
Viral effect churners	1,182,753	i.e. number of people who leave due to recommendation from a person within a social link				
Costs of viral effect in annually	€638,686,850					
Percent of eliminated Alpha1 churn	28%	i.e. percent of Alpha1 users whose churn can be prevented				
Churn campaign target group size	347,200					
Weighted average viral effect	0.175					
Decrease in churn	90,468	i.e. less churners due to the viral effect				
Revenue impact annually	€48,852,597					
Percent of eliminated Alpha2 churn	12%	i.e. percent of Alpha2 users whose churn can be prevented				
Churn campaign target group size	558,000					
Weighted average viral effect	0.179					
Decrease in churn	65,223	i.e. less churners due to the viral effect				
Revenue impact annually	35,220,507					
Total Revenue Increase Annually	**€84,073,103**					
This calculation is a pure network effect, additionally it is possible e.g. focus on Alpha Users in the highest churn risk						
Churn campaign effect Alpha1 vs avegare		6.8	i.e. campaigns to Alpha1 subcribers are this much more effective and to randomly selected subscribers			
Churn campaign effect Alpha2 vs avegare		3.1	i.e. campaigns to Alpha2 subcribers are this much more effective and to randomly selected subscribers			

Social marketing intelligence applied to product marketing for telecoms operators

A mobile operator has 25M subscribers. The operator launches a new product that he expects will generate 3 euro per month in additional revenue per user. They have estimated that 25% of their subscribers are going to take this service.

In this example, we illustrate the viral influence in product marketing. In order to simplify the example, we have made some assumptions based on real customer case data. We assume that 2% of subscribers are top level Alpha Users (Alpha1), i.e. they have 20% viral effect in churn. This means, that if any of Alpha1's take the new service, 20% of their neighbors also take it. We also assume that 10% of the subscribers are lower level influencers (Alpha2). If any of these Alpha2's takes the service, 10% of their neighbors also start to use it. We assume again based on real cases that the churn influence of all other subscribers is 5%.

Ajit Jaokar, Brian Jacobs, Alan Moore and Jouko Ahvenainen

In this example, each Alpha1 has an average 6.0 neighbors over whom they have direct influence in their social network. Similarly, Alpha2 has 4.5 neighbors and other subscribers 1.5 neighbors. We can now calculate that average viral effect for this service is 17.5%. So, in total we can expect approximately 930,000 subscribers to take the service due to the viral effect.

When we know higher influencers (Alpha1 and Alpha2), we can focus the product marketing activities to these subscribers and accelerate the product's adoption. In this example, we are able to get 30% of the Alpha1 to take the service and 10% of Alpha2 to take it. In this way, we can get 63,164 additional subscribers to take it through the viral influence. This means approximately 2.3 million euro in revenue for the operator.

At the same time, the operator is able to achieve the maximum (25%) penetration for the product faster. This means 27 million euro additional revenue. And of course, even more important is that the operator gets higher penetration faster and can become the market leader in the new service area. If the service is a network effect service (service offers more value if it has more users, like a network game or chat), the social influence is even more important.

The calculations are as shown overleaf.

		Editable cells
Number of customers	25,000,000	
Number of Alpha1 Users	500,000	
Number of Alpha2 Users	2,500,000	
Number of Normal Users	22,000,000	
Expected max penetration	25%	
Number of users	6,250,000	
Service ARPU	€3	
Service revenue annually	€225,000,000	
Average viral effect	0.175	
Original adopters	5,318,119	
Viral effect adopters	931,881	i.e. number of people who buy due to recommendation from a person within a social link
Revenue from the viral effect users	*€33,547,723*	
Percent of acquired Alpha1 users	30%	i.e. percent of Alpha1 users who can be acquired to use the service
Marketing campaign target group size	150,000	
Weighted average viral effect	0.182	
Increase in penetration	37,893	i.e. more customers due to the viral effect
Revenue increase annually	*€1,364,146*	
Percent of acquired Alpha2 users	10%	i.e. percent of Alpha2 users who can be acquired to use the service
Marketing campaign target group size	250,000	
Weighted average viral effect	0.180	
Increase in penetration	25,271	i.e. more customers due to the viral effect
Revenue increase annually	909,767	
Revenue increase from higher penetration	*€2,273,913*	
This amount is the pure higher penetration due to the network effect		
Expected time to reach max penetration (months)	18	
Acceleration from the network effect	1.057350554	
Expected time to max penetration with network effect	17.02368238	
Increased revenue due to earlier max penetration	*€27,458,933*	
This is estimated additional revenue from earlier adoptation		
Earlier plus higher penetration revenue boost	**€29,732,846**	i.e. this includes additional revenue from earlier adoptation and higher penetration
Campaign effect Alpha1 vs avegare	**7.4**	i.e. campaigns to Alpha1 subcribers are this much more effective and to randomly selected subscribers
Campaign effect Alpha2 vs avegare	**3.3**	i.e. campaigns to Alpha2 subcribers are this much more effective and to randomly selected subscribers

Social marketing intelligence – BMW

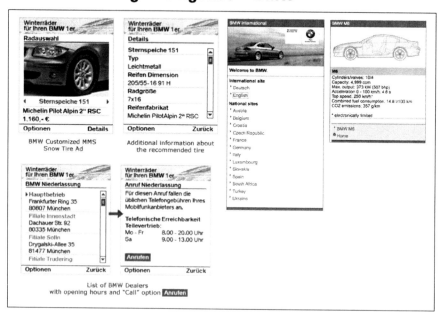

Ajit Jaokar, Brian Jacobs, Alan Moore and Jouko Ahvenainen

BMW used the principles described in this book for a recent mobile campaign. BMW sent an offer via MMS to those BMW customers who had bought a new BMW in the summer months (when no winter tyres are needed). Then, when the first snow fell in Germany, they had a campaign ready to run. The campaign used a customized view of the car model and make that the BMW owner had bought, in the right colour, and onto it, they had fitted (virtually) the recommended winter tyre. Then the BMW owner was invited to hit a link on the phone, to visit the BMW site to see what alternate tyres were available. 30% of those who got the MMS, actually bought winter tyres (and often also new rims) at BMW dealers.

The value proposition works out as follows:

Cost of winter tyres c.	$700
Cost of tyres & rims c.	$2500
Approximate average sale	$1300

Total sales of BMW in summer 2008:	297k
Those sold to hire/fleet:	180k
Total potential customers:	117k
30% response rate =	35,000 customers
Hence, 35,000 customers spending $1300 each =	$45,500,000

And this at a time when new car sales were falling (the total number of cars sold in Germany during 2007 was 3,148,163 – the worst performance since the reunification of Germany in 1990). Given that the cost of the campaign was approximately $60,000 – at German MMS rates, for each MMS sent, the average return on investment was 758 dollars.

Source: http://communities_dominate.blogs.com/brands/2008/09/engagement-ma-1.html? and

http://www.mobiadnews.com/?p=2809#more-2809

Image source: Mobiadnews

Flirtomatic, strongbow man and a free pint of cider!

Vikki Schroder is busy flirting with some fun guys on the Flirtomatic service. For those of you who don't know what Flirtomatic is – it is a mobile flirting service in the UK, which is enormously successful.

Vikki notices a message in her inbox, it is from Strongbow man. Intrigued by Strongbow man, Vikki clicks on the message icon which invites her to visit the bowtime.mobi site. There she sees she can send a message to her flirting pals inviting them to a free pint of Stongbow cider in their nearest pub.

Now Vikki knew that fellow flirters Chris and Tomi both liked a pint, so she decided to send them each a message, which had attached a coupon which was their redemption voucher for their pint of Strongbow.

Chris is finishing work and gets a message from the lovely Vikki. She says, 'Hi there handsome fancy meeting me for a drink, and here's your pint, it's already being poured ;-)xx'

Chris sees that he has an invitation for a refreshing pint of cider, and also an invitation to have a drink with Vikki.

Chris texts her back – 'see you in 50mins at the Dog and Duck ;+) xx'

Amazingly, other users sent Strongbow 70 supersnogs and 929 gifts (although the pint was free to the user, flirting gifts are paid for with

Ajit Jaokar, Brian Jacobs, Alan Moore and Jouko Ahvenainen

flirting points). Strongbow man's profile was rated by 338 users and over 5000 Flirtograms were sent to the Strongbow profile. In fact users treated Strongbow like a real live Flirter. This was a very good example of engagement marketing.

The facts of the case history are that the advertising campaign was directed to selected users, although it was not possible in the beginning to know whether any of these people were interested in Strongbow. Banners and SMS were used to support the campaign. Once at the bow-time.mobi site, the user in exchange for basic information such as a post code, received the coupon that she could send to her friend as a redemption for a free pint.

385,000 branded Strongbow icon gifts sent by Flirtomatic users over mobile

There was a10% click through rate from the gift to bowtime.mobi

Post click objectives were coupon delivery and CRM (delivering an active digital footprint = richer information)

Deploying a social media marketing campaign

Overview

This section brings together all the ideas we have been discussing as we discuss the process of launching a social media marketing campaign. It is important to emphasise that we see the role of social media marketing as encapsulating not just 'social media advertising' but also a wider role including product development, market research etc.

In addition, with an emphasis on data, we have proposed a two-stage approach. First identify the data patterns, and then validate that pattern using specific promotions (which are designed to seek permission from the end consumer). The two-stage approach incorporates the principles of engagement marketing since the promotion we are sending is likely to appeal to the person in the first place, as indicated by our data insights/patterns.

We start a campaign with overview questions like:

- What is the objective? Who are we trying to reach, with what message?
- Which sites should we go on to in order to achieve these objectives?

- What are the deliverables? What outcomes are we hoping to achieve?
- How will we enter? How are we going to engage in the dialogue?
- How will the brand serve the conversation?
- How will we manage the campaign? What are the practicalities?
- How will we monitor progress?
- How will we adjust and correct?
- How will we measure effect at the end of the campaign?
- How will we incorporate feedback into ongoing learning?

There are other broader questions:
- What kind of people normally buy our product?
- What are the reasons for churn?
- In those identified segments within which people don't buy our products, what could we meaningfully offer them? What should be the product features for this segment?

A few initial observations about social media marketing campaigns:
- **Managing the trade-off**: Social media is driven by more than 'shopping'. It is driven by an underlying sense of 'community' which does not necessarily include commerce.
- **The emphasis on metrics**: The emphasis on metrics is important but is not unique to social media marketing campaigns, as we have seen many times in this book. For instance, in academia, the number of papers published is important; in research, the number of patents acquired is important. However, these are not perfect metrics, for instance – many patents are defensive and

hence not a reflection of innovation. However, even within their limitations, metrics are still useful. As a caveat, metrics should be viewed in terms of their utility rather than as raw numbers.

- **Social media marketing incorporates social media advertising**: Social media advertising is all about how can we best construct an advertising campaign so that it is effective within a social media context. This is about targeting the right people with the most appropriate and relevant message (as with all media forms; the difference here is the tightness of the targeting opportunity). Social media marketing on the other hand covers more than social media advertising, for instance the goal of a social media marketing campaign may be to improve a product, or to include users' contributions in product development or planning – otherwise described as harnessing collective intelligence.

- **An emphasis on data:** There are different ways in which we could engage with online social media. In a specific case, we could work with a designated online social network. In the widest sense, we have to consider a converged scenario. By 'converged scenario', we mean a combination of Web, Media and Telecoms. There are two elements that are common to these platforms: first, the underlying transactional data and secondly, working within the concept of the customer 'conversation'. Thus, the two common elements of social media marketing are: The conversation and the data.

- **The metaphor:** Air traffic controller or focus group? Most marketers are used to focus groups, a controlled discussion as a means of generating feedback from people they think are relevant and specific to their key audience. However, that does not reflect the true nature of a marketer's interaction with social media conversations today. A more appropriate metaphor is that of an air traffic controller. An air traffic controller simultaneously monitors a number of rapidly changing real time scenarios and reacts quickly, making small incremental changes to a changing pattern whilst keeping the overall goal in mind. In a similar way, we see the marketer of the future monitoring a dashboard (real time data feeds) and making small, incremental tweaks based on a number of inputs. The results of the changes are benchmarked against sales, industry standards and other parameters.

Managing the social media advertising campaign
What is a social media marketing campaign?
To summarise our previous discussions, we describe a social media marketing campaign as follows:

- A mechanism to interact with a set of digital socially networked conversations from a marketing perspective.
- Based on converged media (since conversations span technologies and media).
- Measurable via a set of social media metrics.
- These metrics function as the proverbial 'air traffic control' monitoring the domain in almost real time.
- Based on the data driven dials of this interface, the marketer monitors these 'many way conversations'. Many way

  Ajit Jaokar, Brian Jacobs, Alan Moore and Jouko Ahvenainen

conversations take place between users but also between the marketer and the user.

- Based on insights gathered from data, the marketer validates these insights using specific promotions which seek to gain permission for an ongoing engagement with the user.
- The marketer benchmarks the insights gained from these conversations against a set of transactional data (sales, surveys etc) to monitor and tweak a series of narrowcast (or long tail) campaigns.
- Thus, instead of having one large 'broadcast' campaign – we have many small narrowcast, interactive and ongoing campaigns.
- The campaigns and conversations are based on a feedback loop hence they are iterative and form an ongoing learning experience.
- The goals of a social media marketing campaign include advertising but can also be extended to cover product development, trend monitoring, market research, reducing churn, benchmarking and so on.

We depict an overview of a social media marketing campaign overleaf.

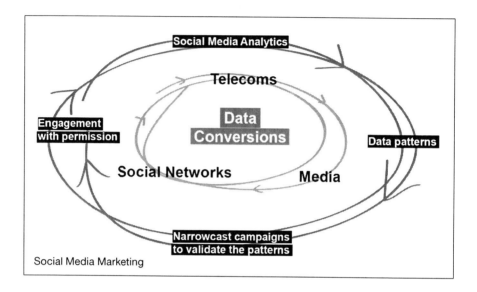

Social Media Marketing

What is the 'brief' – what is the campaign going to achieve?
We have seen before that the goals of a social media marketing campaign may be different from those of a traditional advertising campaign (for instance – by definition, a social media advertising campaign is 'two way' as opposed to a traditional marketing campaign which (in most cases) is 'one way').

Because a social media campaign may be emergent (its goal may not be known in advance), we expect that a social media campaign will start off with a broad goal – but the specifics of that goal will evolve and will refine with iterations and by the understanding that emerges from an analyses of the underlying data. The conversation itself is not unidirectional – but multidirectional and multidimensional. Conversations exist not only between the marketer and the user, but also between users. Besides targeted advertising, the goals of a social media campaign could include new product development, benchmarking, reducing churn, market research, tracking emerging trends and the like.

Starting with the conversation

Any social media marketing campaign starts with a conversation, and with the marketer seeking to engage with that conversation. Like any conversation, its direction is unpredictable – an aspect that most marketers are not comfortable with. In many cases, the users may change the message of the advertisement itself – for example by creating alternate YouTube videos of the campaign. Also, conversations span technologies and platforms, they may take place on the Web, in traditional media spaces or within telecoms.

How will the brand serve the conversation?

The first question in engaging with the conversation is for the marketer to ask himself: How will the brand serve the conversation?

There are three possibilities (and of course combinations thereof):

a) By **providing information**: An example of providing information is the Being a Girl[96] site created by the makers of Tampax[97]. The site talks of the many aspects of growing up rather than discussing the specifics of the product.

b) By **providing entertainment**: The Sony Bravia ad[98] is an example of entertainment combined with advertising (essentially a whole song played over the backdrop of the famous ad featuring the dropping of thousands of multicoloured balls down the streets of San Francisco)

c) By **being a 'cause'**: The top 10 viral advertisements of all

---

96   http://www.beinggirl.com/
97   www.tampax.com
98   http://en.wikipedia.org/wiki/BRAVIA

times[99] lists the campaign for Dove evolution [100] which used time-lapse photography to show the transformation of a normal woman into a billboard model using beauty stylists and Photoshop enhancements. The clip was released under the slogan 'No wonder our perception of real beauty is distorted'. The communication (and indeed the whole cause notion) fitted within the Dove 'Campaign for Real Beauty' idea.

What to measure?

We have seen before that the end goal of a social media campaign may be different than that of a traditional campaign. A social media marketing campaign facilitates and engages with conversations on an ongoing basis in a feedback loop. The end goal of a social media metric will be to facilitate and monitor conversations. The conversations we monitor could be at the brand level and also at the product-category level.

Thus, the characteristics of a social media metric include:
a) Social media metrics monitor social media campaigns (described above).
b) Social media metrics are based on the concept of a feedback loop, an iterative improvement of the campaign and the usage of data patterns which are validated by specific promotions.
c) Social media metrics could be predictive; they could be used for measuring future trends.
d) Social media metrics may be emergent, they could start off by monitoring a specific aspect but evolve further from that role.

---

99   http://business.timesonline.co.uk/tol/business/industry_sectors/media/article2138718.ece
100 http://www.campaignforrealbeauty.com/flat4.asp?id=6909

Ajit Jaokar, Brian Jacobs, Alan Moore and Jouko Ahvenainen

e) Managing data is an important element of social media metrics.

f) Social media metrics are likely to monitor conversations across different platforms as the smallest unit of interaction.

g) A social media metric may be used for functions other than advertisements; for example for product development, spotting trends, benchmarking against surveys etc.

h) Social media metrics are likely to be used in long tail, narrow-cast campaigns.

i) Data used in social media campaigns may have to be comple-mented from other market research data to get an accurate picture.

Micro segment the campaign (Narrowcast)

A social media advertising campaign is likely to be long tail and narrowcast working with many niches rather than one specific monolithic audience.

The data

Since data is an important element of a social media marketing campaign, the question arises: where do we get data from? There are many sources – some of which include:

a) Directly engaging with social networks

b) Working with sites like YouTube and Flickr

c) Working with telecoms operators or mobile social networks

d) Crawling the Web (writing a program to access the Web)

e) By working with actual customer data and loading it into a data-base and processing it for the metrics

f) Through an organisation's various customer touchpoints

The Mechanics

The actual mechanics of running a social media marketing campaign should consider the following factors:

- Real time: The feedback loop for the campaign should be real time or close to real time. Real time feedback is one of the key differentiators for social media and designing the campaign for real time analysis is a key factor within the planning of social media advertising

- Privacy: The social media campaign should work within privacy rules, regulations and guidelines, and should always be transparent in its actions

- Trust: The social media advertising campaign should engender trust. Trust flows both ways. Users should trust the marketer not to be engaged in SPAM, to respect their privacy etc – but the marketer should also trust users to 'modify' their message – which may well happen. The marketer should also value the user's feedback and respect it

- Mutability: The 'audience' is not passive. In fact, members may mutate your product and create 'alternate' digital versions of your product some of which may not be flattering to you!

- Engagement: Both at a brand level and at a product level. Engagement alone is not enough – we need to be able to quantify engagement through metrics

- Narrowcast and long tail: The social media marketing campaign may actually be a set of many mini-campaigns designed around the metrics

 Ajit Jaokar, Brian Jacobs, Alan Moore and Jouko Ahvenainen

- Supplementing of data: The data used in social media marketing campaigns may need to be enriched from other sources
- Accountability: Because social media marketing campaigns are likely to be based on niche segments (long Tail), they are likely to be oriented towards higher value items. By the same token, they are also likely to favour mobile social networks because the closed loop principle works well with mobile campaigns
- Data oriented and two-phase: The campaign may be based on data patterns which may be validated by specific promotions

Goals of the campaign

The goals for a social media advertising campaign could include:

- Targeted advertising – for instance working with Alpha users
- Benchmarking: Against surveys, sales etc
- Product development: New and ongoing products
- Forecasting: Short term and long term trends
- Churn reduction
- Viral marketing (user get user campaigns, for instance)
- There is also the option to directly work with Alpha Users. For instance, the association of Motorola and Pepsi with the Back Dorm boys in China – when Motorola and Pepsi sponsored their music/act on the web

Manage the feedback loop

Finally, we need to treat the whole process as an ongoing feedback loop where we listen to the users with humility and sometimes with a sense of fun!

Why now – in a recession?

As we write this book (late in 2008), we are facing a recession. In an article called *Dude, where is my Ad?* [101], Om Malik points to the forthcoming difficulties in the advertising model. In it, he says that: ***The only ad-related company that looks like somewhat of a safe place amidst this chaos is Google (GOOG), thanks largely to its performance based advertising system, which allows advertisers to only pay for what brings them returns.***

This interactivity and accountability has always been an issue for traditional media forms (despite the heroic work of generations of analysts and econometricians, those of us involved have to admit that we have to a large extent failed to move CFO's and CEO's away from a sense that advertising is a cost not an investment). With the recession looming,, interactivity and accountability (monitoring the action to the advertisement or closing the loop) are likely to be even more important.

We foresee that this drive towards accountability and the speed of reaction will help social media marketing become an important avenue for advertisers because it offers so much more than conventional forms of advertising. We see social media marketing as a complement to, as opposed to a replacement for more conventional marketing forms – as a component of campaigns that will only grow in importance and

---

101 http://www.businessweek.com/technology/content/oct2008/tc20081010_137369.htm?campaign_id=rss_daily

significance over time. But brand marketers have to understand that placing the old furniture of advertising within any form of socially net-worked environment, where the reasons that people come in the first place is to communicate with each other, is only going to result in dimin-ishing returns.

Drilling for oil:
The significance of data

We started this book with a discussion on community, conversations and data – and that's a good place to conclude this book as well.

With the proliferation of online social networks, concepts like social media, social media content (or user-generated content), Web 2.0 and digitally connected communities are becoming a part of our vocabulary. We shouldn't be surprised by these developments, as, after all, communities preceded technology; in fact they really mark the beginning of civilisation. As we've seen, humans are a 'WE SPECIES', a social and networking specie. We have an innate need to connect and to communicate. That is why social networking in all its forms is thriving.

Mass media communications, such as television, newspapers, magazines are in fact a poor substitute for meaningful two-way interaction, argued cultural theorist Raymond Williams who developed a point of view that minority ownership of the mass media was a perversion of communication and the needs of human beings. He concluded that minority ownership, with its own particular interests led ultimately to a corruption of a necessary resource for a vibrant culture and democratic society.

188

MIT Professor, Henry Jenkins in 'Convergence Culture' believes that convergence is a cultural rather than a technological process. We now live in a world where every story, image, sound, idea, brand, and relationship will play itself out across all possible media platforms. In a networked society, people are increasingly forming knowledge communities to pool information and work together to solve problems they could not confront individually

Against this backdrop, traditional media companies, businesses of all shapes and sizes, and all aspects of, marketing are exploring avenues by which they can work with social media. This book offers one way of looking at the world and interpreting it. We have adopted an interdisciplinary approach, with authors from a background in Research, Advertising, Media and Data Analysis. We have also approached social media marketing from three distinct but interrelated perspectives, the Web (including social media), Telecoms (including mobile) and Media.

These perspectives are interconnected and are based on data and conversations. Our approach is data driven. It is also based on convergence (Web/Mobile/Telecoms and Media). In this sense, it differs from other complimentary approaches due to its emphasis on data and convergence. Many of the social relationships / behavioural analysis can be inferred from underlying data. In fact, it is more insightful to derive relationships from the underlying data rather than from explicitly stated relationships.

Ajit Jaokar, Brian Jacobs, Alan Moore and Jouko Ahvenainen

Any body of transactional data derived from participants in an electronic conversation can be viewed as a social network (such as email data, telecoms call records, instant messaging data, forum posts etc). This idea forms a key principle in our research behind this book. Data and privacy form the bedrock of this multi-way conversation between the marketer and the participants. Ultimately, we see the participants and the marketer enter into a trusted relationship based on transparency where the participants share data about themselves and entrust the marketer with their data in return for better and personalised services.

Finally, social media and social media marketing are emerging topics. As we had mentioned in the foreword of the book, we do not claim to have all the answers and we welcome all your comments. You can contact us through the web site www.social-media-marketing-community.com . Please contact Ajit Jaokar ajit.jaokar@future-text.com for a copy of our research on which some of the ideas underlying this book are based and also if you wish to get any more case studies included in future editions of this book.

Appendix:
Social network analysis

This section is derived from wikipedia and explains social network analysis concepts.[102]

A social network is a social structure made of nodes (which are generally individuals or organizations) that are tied by one or more specific types of interdependency, such as values, visions, ideas, financial exchange, friendship, kinship, dislike, conflict or trade. The resulting graph-based structures are often very complex.

Social network analysis views social relationships in terms of nodes and ties. Nodes are the individual actors within the networks, and ties are the relationships between the actors. There can be many kinds of ties between the nodes. Research in a number of academic fields has shown that social networks operate on many levels, from families up to the level of nations, and play a critical role in determining the way problems are solved, organizations are run, and the degree to which individuals succeed in achieving their goals.

In its simplest form, a social network is a map of all of the relevant ties between the nodes being studied. The network can also be used

---

102 http://en.wikipedia.org/wiki/Social_network

to determine the social capital of individual actors. These concepts are often displayed in a social network diagram, where nodes are the points and ties are the lines.

Social network analysis (related to network theory) has emerged as a key technique in modern sociology, anthropology, sociolinguistics, geography, social psychology, communication studies, information science, organizational studies, economics, and biology as well as a popular topic of speculation and study.

People have used the social network metaphor for over a century to connote complex sets of relationships between members of social systems at all scales, from interpersonal to international. Social network analysis has now moved from being a suggestive metaphor to an analytic approach to a paradigm, with its own theoretical statements, methods, social network analysis software, and researchers. Rather than treating individuals (persons, organizations, states) as discrete units of analysis, it focuses on how the structure of ties affects individuals and their relationships. In contrast to analyses that assume that socialization into norms determines behavior, network analysis looks to see the extent to which the structure and composition of ties affect norms.

The power of social network analysis stems from its difference from traditional social scientific studies, which assume that it is the attributes of individual actors – whether they are friendly or unfriendly, smart or dumb, etc. – that matter. Social network analysis produces an alternate view, where the attributes of individuals are less important than their relationships and ties with other actors within the network. This approach has turned out to be useful for explaining many real-world phenomena, but leaves less room for individual agency, the ability for

Ajit Jaokar, Brian Jacobs, Alan Moore and Jouko Ahvenainen

individuals to influence their success, because so much of it rests within the structure of their network.

Social networks have also been used to examine how organizations interact with each other, characterizing the many informal connections that link executives together, as well as associations and connections between individual employees at different organizations. For example, power within organizations often comes more from the degree to which an individual within a network is at the center of many relationships than actual job title.

Metrics (measures) in social network analysis

- Betweenness: The extent to which a nodes lies between other nodes in the network. This measure takes into account the connectivity of the node's neighbors, giving a higher value for nodes which bridge clusters. The measure reflects the number of people who a person is connecting indirectly through their direct links.
- Bridge: An edge is said to be a bridge if deleting it would cause its endpoints to lie in different components of a graph.
- Centrality: This measure gives rough indication of the social power of a node based on how well they "connect" the network. "Betweeness", "Closeness", and "Degree" are all measures of centrality.
- Closeness: The degree an individual is near all other individuals in a network (directly or indirectly). It reflects the ability to access information through the "grapevine" of network members. Thus, closeness is the inverse of the sum of the shortest distances between each individual and every other person in the network.
- Clustering coefficient: A measure of the likelihood that two asso-

ciates of a node are associates themselves. A higher clustering coefficient indicates a greater 'cliquishness'.

- Cohesion: The degree to which actors are connected directly to each other by cohesive bonds. Groups are identified as 'cliques' if every individual is directly tied to every other individual, 'social circles' if there is less stringency of direct contact, which is imprecise, or as structurally cohesive blocks if precision is wanted.
- Degree: The count of the number of ties to other actors in the network. See also degree (graph theory).
- Eigenvector centrality : A measure of the importance of a node in a network. It assigns relative scores to all nodes in the network based on the principle that connections to nodes having a high score contribute more to the score of the node in question.
- Prestige: In a directed graph prestige is the term used to describe a node's centrality. "Degree Prestige", "Proximity Prestige", and "Status Prestige" are all measures of Prestige. See also degree (graph theory).
- Radiality: Degree an individual's network reaches out into the network and provides novel information and influence.
- Reach: The degree any member of a network can reach other members of the network.
- Structural cohesion: The minimum number of members who, if removed from a group, would disconnect the group.
- Structural equivalence: Refers to the extent to which nodes have a common set of linkages to other nodes in the system. The nodes don't need to have any ties to each other to be structurally equivalent.

Appendix:
Research papers references

- Extracting reputation in multi agent systems by means of social network topology – Joseph Pujol et al
- Authoritative Sources in a Hyperlinked Environment – Jon M. Kleinberg
- Introduction to Social Network Methods – Robert A. Hanneman Department of Sociology
- University of California, Riverside 2001
- Inside Social Network Analysis – Kate Ehrlich1 and Inga Carboni2
- A p2p global trust model based on recommendation – zhen zhang1, xiao-ming wang1, yun-xiao wang
- The EigenTrust Algorithm for Reputation Management in P2P Networks Sepandar D. Kamvar et al
- Decentralized Trust Management Matt Blaze Joan Feigenbaum Jack Lacy AT&T Research Murray Hill, NJ 07974
- Analysis of Social Voting Patterns on Digg Kristina Lerman and Aram Galstyan University of Southern California Information Sciences Institute

- Distributed Uniform Sampling in Real-World Networks Asad Awan Ronaldo A. Ferreira Suresh Jagannathan Ananth Grama Department of Computer Sciences Purdue University
- Accuracy of Metrics for Inferring Trust and Reputation in Semantic Web-based Social Networks Jennifer Golbeck, James Hendler
- Email networks and the spread of computer viruses M. E. J. Newman, Stephanie Forrest, and Justin Balthrop
- Sybilproof Reputation Mechanisms Alice Cheng Center for Applied Mathematics Cornell University
- Effective Use of Reputation in Peer-to-Peer Environments – Thanasis G. Papaioannou and George D. Stamoulis Department of Informatics, Athens University of Economics and Business (AUEB) Athens, Greece.
- Exploiting Social Networks for Internet Search Alan Mislove Krishna P. Gummadi Peter Druschel
- Poking Facebook: Characterization of OSN Applications Minas Gjoka, Michael Sirivianos, Athina Markopoulou, Xiaowei Yang University of California, Irvine
- Growth of the Flickr Social Network – Alan Mislove et al
- Characterizing Social Cascades in Flickr Meeyoung Cha et al
- Goodbye Pareto Principle, Hello Long Tail: The Effect of Search Costs on the Concentration of Product Sales – Erik Brynjolfsson, Yu (Jeffrey) Hu , Duncan Simester
- Vizster: Visualizing Online Social Networks Jeffrey Heer, danah boyd

- Trust and Reputation Model in Peer-to-Peer Networks Yao Wang, Julita Vassileva
- Measurement and Analysis of Online Social Networks Alan Mislove et al
- Inferring vertex properties from topology in large networks – Janne Aukia
- Inferring vertex properties from topology in large networks Janne Sinkkonen et al
- From Niches to Riches: The Anatomy of the Long Tail – Sloan Management Review Erik Brynjolfsson, Yu 'Jeffrey' Hu, Michael D. Smith
- In the next episode, entertainment will be circular – Nokia
- PeerTrust: Supporting Reputation-Based Trust for Peer-to-Peer Electronic Communities Li Xiong and Ling Liu
- Digital Footprints Online identity management and search in the age of transparency Mary Madden, Susannah Fox, Aaron Smith, Jessica Vitak Pew Internet report
- NOYB: Privacy in Online Social Networks Saikat Guha, Kevin Tang, and Paul Francis
- Characterizing Privacy in Online Social Networks Balachander Krishnamurthy, Craig E. Wills
- Bayesian clustering of huge friendship networks Janne Aukia – Helsinki University of technology
- Propagation Models for Trust and Distrust in Social Networks Cai-Nicolas Ziegler and Georg Lausen
- Reputation and Social Network Analysis in Multi-Agent Systems Jordi Sabater et al

- Structure and Evolution of Online Social Networks Ravi Kumar Jasmine Novak Andrew Tomkins Yahoo! Research
- TRUST MANAGEMENT THROUGH REPUTATION MECHA-NISMS GIORGOS ZACHARIA and PATTIE MAES MIT Media Laboratory, Cambridge MA, U.S.A.
- Trust Networks on the Semantic Web Jennifer Golbeck, Bijan Parsia, and James Hendler
- Trust Propagation in Small Worlds Elizabeth Gray, Jean-Marc Seigneur, Yong Chen, and Christian Jensen
- A Few Chirps About Twitter Balachander Krishnamurthy, Phillipa Gill, Martin Arlitt
- Cooperative Peer Groups in NICE Seungjoon Lee Rob Sherwood Bobby Bhattacharjee
- A survey of trust and reputation systems for online service provision Audun Jøsang, Roslan Ismail , Colin Boyd
- A Comparison of Sampling Techniques for Web Graph Characterization Luca Becchetti Carlos Castillo Debora Donato Adriano Fazzone
- Analysis of Topological Characteristics of Huge Online Social Networking Services Yong Yeo Ahn et al
- Are You Moved by Your Social Network Application? Abderrahmen Mtibaa, Augustin Chaintreau, Jason LeBrun, Earl Oliver, Anna-Kaisa Pietilainen, Christophe Diot
- Community structure in social and biological networks Michelle Girvan1, and M. E. J. Newman
- Component models for large networks Janne Sinkkonen Helsinki University of Technology

 Ajit Jaokar, Brian Jacobs, Alan Moore and Jouko Ahvenainen

- Trust Propagation in Small Worlds Elizabeth Gray, Jean-Marc Seigneur, Yong Chen, and Christian Jensen
- A Trust Evaluation Framework in Distributed Networks: Vulnerability Analysis and Defense Against Attacks Yan Lindsay Sun, Zhu Hany, Wei Yuy and K. J. Ray Liuy
- Analyzing the Structure and Evolution of Massive Telecom Graphs Amit A. Nanavati, Rahul Singh, Dipanjan Chakraborty, Koustuv Dasgupta , Sougata Mukherjea, Gautam Das, Siva Gurumurthy, Anupam Joshi
- Trust-Aware Collaborative Filtering for Recommender Systems Paolo Massa and Paolo Avesani
- Geographic routing in social networks David Liben-Nowell, Jasmine Novak, Ravi Kumar, Prabhakar Raghavan, and Andrew Tomkins
- Graph Mining Approaches for the Discovery of Web Communities Tsuyoshi Murata
- Group Formation in Large Social Networks: Membership, Growth, and Evolution Lars Backstrom, Dan Huttenlocher, Jon Kleinberg, Xiangyang Lan
- Instant Messaging Worms Propagation Simulation and Countermeasures HU Huaping, WEI Jianli
- Inferring Binary Trust Relationships in Web-Based Social Networks JENNIFER GOLBECK and JAMES HENDLER
- The mathematics of networks M. E. J. Newman
- Measurement and Analysis of Online Social Networks Alan Mislove, Massimiliano Marcon, Krishna P. Gummadi, Peter Druschel, Bobby Bhattacharjee

- Mining Knowledge-Sharing Sites for Viral Marketing Matthew Richardson and Pedro Domingos
- Mining Knowledge-Sharing Sites for Viral Marketing Matthew Richardson and Pedro Domingos
- RE: Reliable Email Scott Garriss, Michael Kaminsky, Michael J. Freedman, Brad Karp, David Mazières, Haifeng Yu
- Reputation Network Analysis for Email Filtering Jennifer Golbeck, James Hendler
- The pagerank algorithm
- Trawling the Web for emerging cyber-communities Ravi Kumar, Prabhakar Raghavan, Sridhar Rajagopalan, Andrew Tomkins
- Accuracy of Metrics for Inferring Trust and Reputation in Semantic Web-based Social Networks Jennifer Golbeck, James Hendler
- I Tube, You Tube, Everybody Tubes: Analyzing the World's Largest User Generated Content Video System Meeyoung Cha, Hae-woon Kwak, Pablo Rodriguez, Yong-Yeol Ahn, and Sue Moon Telefonica Research, Barcelona
- YouTube Traffic Characterization: A View From the Edge Phillipa Gill, Martin Arlittz, Zongpeng Li, Anirban Mahantix

 Ajit Jaokar, Brian Jacobs, Alan Moore and Jouko Ahvenainen

About the authors

Ajit Jaokar

Ajit Jaokar is the founder of the London based publishing and research company futuretext focussed on emerging Web and Mobile technologies. His thinking is widely followed in the industry and his blog, The OpenGardensBlog, was recently rated a top 20 wireless blog worldwide.

Ajit plays an advisory and a consulting role to a range of organizations globally. He has worked with The European Union, Telecoms Operators, Device manufacturers, social networking companies and security companies in various strategic and visionary roles.

His recent talks and forthcoming talks include:
- CEBIT 2009
- Keynote at O Reilly Web20 expo (April 2007);
- MobileWorld Congress (2007 and 2008);
- Keynote at Java One
  (Ex-Motorola CTO Padmasree Warrior's panel);
- European Parliament – Brussels – (Electronic Internet Foundation);
- Stanford University's Digital visions program;

- MIT Sloan;
- Fraunhofer FOKUS – Talk on Mobility, Web 2.0 and Identity;
- University of St. Gallen (Switzerland) – invited to speak about emerging trends in Mobility and new media;
- Mobile Web Strategies (partner event of CTIA in San Francisco)

His existing books include Mobile Web 2.0 and OpenGardens.

Technical presentations have included
- IMS World in Monaco;
- Ajax world in Santa Clara and New York.
- Various at Fraunhofer Institute

Media appearances include
- BBC – Newsnight – 3phone launch;
- CNN money;
- BBC digital planet

Ajit chairs Oxford University's Next generation mobile applications panel and conducts a course on Web 2.0 and User generated content at Oxford University.

Ajit lives in London, UK, but has three nationalities (British, Indian and New Zealander) and is proud of all three. He is currently doing a PhD on Identity and Reputation systems at UCL in London

Brian Jacobs, Director, BJ&A Ltd.

Brian Jacobs has spent over 38 years in advertising and media agencies, at Leo Burnett (where he was UK Media Director, European Media Director, both based in London, and International Media Director, based in Chicago); at Carat International, (Managing Director), and at Universal McCann (EMEA Regional Director). In 2003 he joined Millward Brown (part of WPP's Kantar Group), where he set up and established that organisation's Global Media Practice.

Brian Jacobs started his career in media research before moving into media planning and management. Over his career, he has worked for many leading marketers, including Coca-Cola, Procter & Gamble, McDonald's, Kellogg's, Nestle, Volkswagen, and Unilever.

Brian started Brian Jacobs and Associates Ltd (BJ&A), a virtual communications consultancy (www.bjanda.com) in 2006. Since launch, BJ&A's clients have included Johnson and Johnson, Bacardi Global Brands, The Newspaper Marketing Agency, Initiative, the computer games start-up Supermassive Games, the analytics business Xtract and the buzz monitoring service, Whitevector.

Brian Jacobs is a regular contributor to conferences and to trade papers. He is co-author, with the late Dr Simon Broadbent of the UK standard text on media planning, buying and research: 'Spending Advertising Money'.

Brian was voted a Fellow of the UK Institute of Practitioners in Advertising in 1985.

Alan Moore.

Alan Moore is the co-author of Communities Dominate Brands: Business and Marketing Challenges for the 21st Century. The founder of the communication consultancy SMLXL, Alan is the originator of the term, philosophy, and principles of Engagement Marketing and Communications. His writing and work has provided an international platform for him to address radio, television, conference, and digital audiences globally.

He is an executive director of Mass Niche Media, a board director of the Social Marketing Intelligence Company Xtract (http://xtract.com), and sits on the advisory board of the IPR and patent company CVON. He has taught mobile commerce and communications at the Oxford University for Continuing Education.

SMLXL has extensive knowledge and experience in how to engage and inspire people and companies with the possibilities of Engagement Marketing. SMLXL enables companies and brands to better engage with each other. For example, Alan has been credited with having a significant influence on how Nokia has evolved its practice of marketing towards a more engaged approach. Alan's unique experience enables him to provide inspiration and strategies for how businesses can prepare themselves for the challenges ahead, driven by the evolution of media, technology, communications, and commerce.

　　　Ajit Jaokar, Brian Jacobs, Alan Moore and Jouko Ahvenainen

Jouko Ahvenainen

Jouko Ahvenainen (www.joukoahvenainen.com) is Co-founder of Xtract Ltd. Jouko has 15 years experience in international business management. Before his serial entrepreneur career Jouko held progressively senior positions at diverse technology firms including Cap Gemini Ernst & Young, Powerwave Technologies Inc., Nokia, and Sonera in various sales, executive and management consulting positions. In all roles he has been a key driver to create new business.

He is one of the pioneers in social media marketing, and personally had significant role to develop and sell the first social marketing intelligence solutions for mobile and media companies. He has also large traditional marketing experience, starting from some well known political campaigns in mid 1990's. Jouko has vast experience of international business in Asia, Europe, and North America; he has lived and worked in Finland, Malaysia, UK, and the U.S.

Jouko has worked in teams to close several VC deals (from 150k USD to 15M USD), and also closed many large customer deals and been responsible for 40M USD annual revenue. He started his first own software business when he was 16-year-old. Jouko also serves as a Senior Partner at Replicon, a financial and business services company, where he is also a Certified Adviser in Nasdaq OMX First North list at Helsinki and Stockholm stock exchanges. Jouko is on the boards of various start-up companies, and is a co-founder or seed investor in six companies (e.g. www.growvc.com).

Jouko is a regular speaker in many marketing, start-up funding, mobile and web 2.0 conferences including Mobile World Congress (Barcelona), CTIA (San Francisco), and several Informa's, IIR's and others' conferences around Europe, Asia, and the US.

Jouko lives near London. He holds an MBA from Helsinki School of Economics, a joint program with McCombs School of Business, at the University of Texas, Austin and a M.Sc.(Tech.) from Helsinki University of Technology.

Printed in the United Kingdom by
Lightning Source UK Ltd., Milton Keynes
138513UK00001B/10/P